Washington, D.C.

Washington, D.C.

R. Conrad Stein

Children's Press®
A Division of Grolier Publishing
New York London Hong Kong Sydney

Frontispiece: The Jefferson Memorial

Front cover: The U.S. Capitol

Back cover: Historic rowhouses

Consultant: Matthew Gilmore, Washingtoniana Department, District of Columbia Public Library

Please note: All statistics are as up-to-date as possible at the time of publication.

Visit Children's Press on the Internet at http://publishing.grolier.com

Book production by Editorial Directions, Inc.

Library of Congress Cataloging-in-Publication Data

Stein, R. Conrad.
Washington, D.C. / by R. Conrad Stein.
    144 p. 24 cm.— (America the beautiful. Second series)
Includes bibliographical references and index.
Summary : An introduction to the geography, natural resources, history, economy,
important sites, and people of the District of Columbia.
    ISBN 0-516-21046-7
    1. Washington (D.C.)—Juvenile literature. I. Title. II. Series.
F194.3.S72 2000
975.3—dc21   98-54910
                                                                              CIP
                                                                               AC

Acknowledgments

The author wishes to thank the men and women of the District of Columbia Public Library for their part in preserving the history of the capital city.

Lincoln Memorial

National Air and Space Museum

Georgetown

George
Washington

Contents

Mount Vernon

The Metro

July 4th celebration

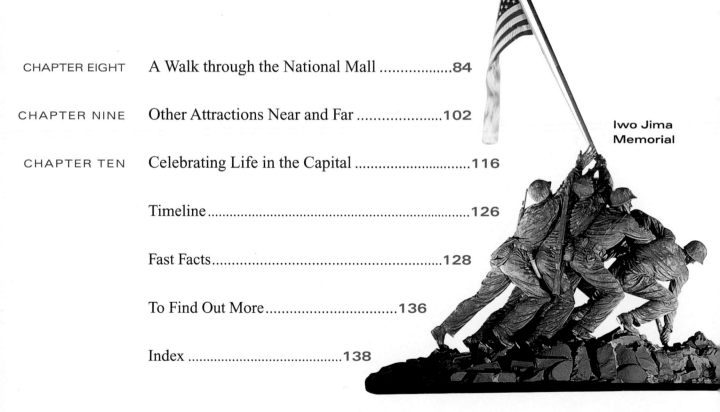

Iwo Jima
Memorial

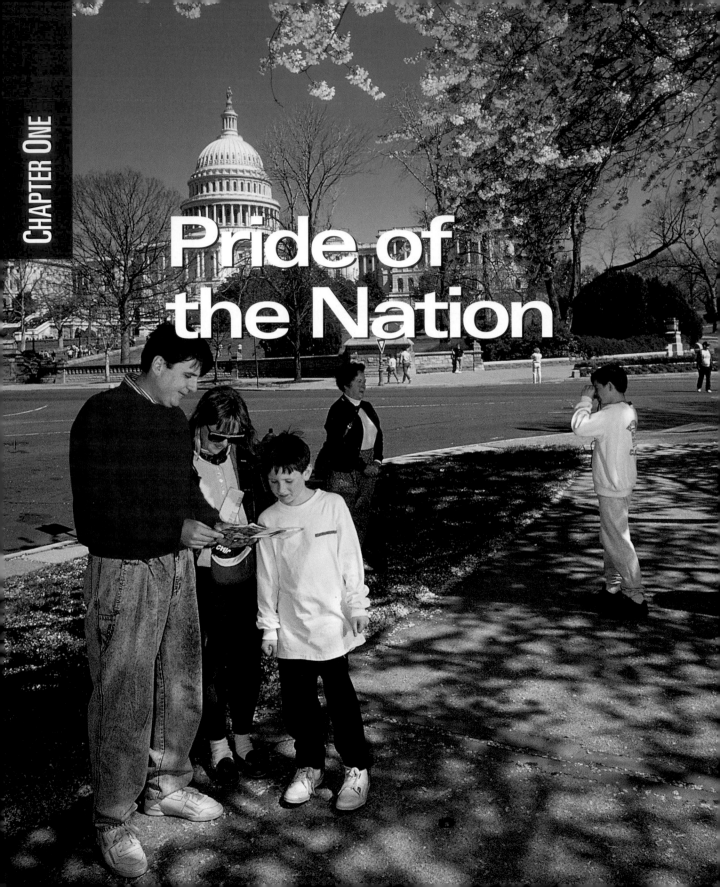

CHAPTER ONE

Pride of
the Nation

A movie called *Mr. Smith Goes to Washington* tells the story of a naive young man who is selected to become a U.S. senator. Early in the film, the man tours Washington, D.C., on a bus. He is overwhelmed at seeing the White House, the Capitol, the Lincoln Memorial, the Washington Monument, and other marvels of the city. Later, Mr. Smith heroically exposes a corrupt fellow senator from his own state.

James Stewart in *Mr. Smith Goes to Washington*

Mr. Smith Goes to Washington was a popular movie when it was released in 1939. But many viewers today dismiss the film's story as being overly sentimental and its message as hopelessly old-fashioned. Yet the scene where the new senator is awestruck by the sights of Washington, D.C., is as modern as tomorrow. First-time visitors to Washington still get goosebumps when they see the glories of the U.S. capital.

There is no city anywhere quite like Washington, D.C. It is one of the few large cities in the world that was designed before it was built. With its broad boulevards, outdoor statues, fountains, and grand public buildings, Washington is certainly one of the most beautiful cities on Earth. Its outstanding collection of museums

Opposite: Tourists enjoying Washington, D.C., with the cherry trees in bloom

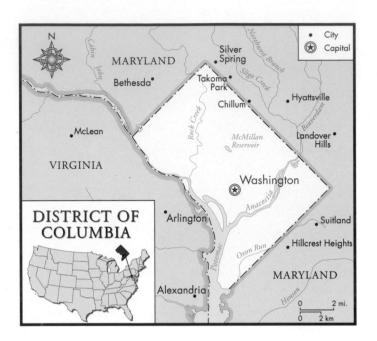

Geopolitical map of Washington, D.C.

also excites visitors. And, in many respects, Washington is the world's most important city. It is the center of government of the mightiest country on Earth. Decisions made by leaders in Washington affect not only the lives of people in the United States but also those of people in other nations.

About 4 million people live in Washington, D.C., and its suburbs. The suburban communities spread into the states of Virginia and Maryland. Washington is the only city in the nation that is not a part of any state. The capital lies within a segment of land that is administered by the federal government and called the District of Columbia (D.C.).

Every year, millions of people visit Washington, D.C. Most tourists go to the historic city center. They walk wonderstruck through the parklike National Mall, which is flanked by museum buildings and monuments. They gaze in awe at the Washington Monument, the famous symbol of the city. Touring the capital, a visitor is quick to understand a statement expressed by Mr. Smith in that long-ago movie: "I don't think I've ever been so thrilled in my whole life."

The Washington Monument is one of the best-known sites in the city.

CHAPTER TWO

The Federal City

The United States emerged as a nation after the Revolutionary War (1775–1783). The conflict allowed the original thirteen colonies to break free from Great Britain. During and immediately after the war, the United States had no permanent capital city. Philadelphia had served as a temporary capital through most of the war years, and George Washington, the first president, took his oath of office in New York City. Clearly, the country needed a place for government representatives to assemble and a place to hold national celebrations. From the earliest discussions, it was suggested that such a future capital be named Washington, after the first president. Initially, the proposed capital was simply called the Federal City.

The capital city was named for President George Washington.

A Site in the Wilderness

Where should the infant nation put its seat of government? Even before the country's birth, northern states and southern states bickered over many things, including the location of their capital. The northerners wanted to establish the capital in Philadelphia, which they thought of as the country's most sophisticated city. The southern states objected because Philadelphia was a stronghold of the Quaker religion, and Quakers were staunch enemies of slavery.

Opposite: Old Georgetown in the early 1880s

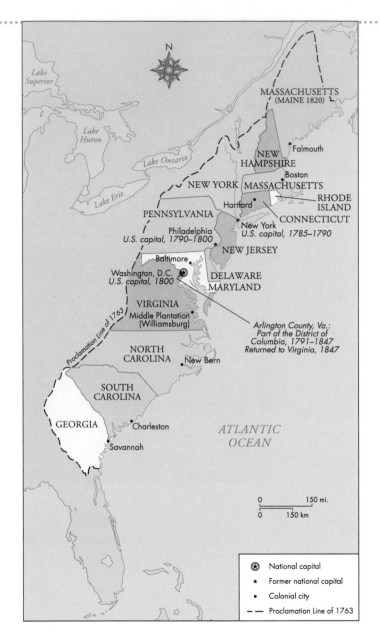

The thirteen colonies and Washington, D.C.

A compromise was worked out in 1789 when two statesmen, Thomas Jefferson and Alexander Hamilton, met at a New York City restaurant. Jefferson, from Virginia, argued that if the capital were placed in the south, the southern states would willingly pay their war debts to the federal government. Hamilton, from New York, agreed to a southern location. Congress determined the Federal City should be built along the Potomac River in the states of Maryland and Virginia, and President George Washington was given the authority to choose the exact spot.

George Washington was born and grew up in Virginia near the Potomac River. For the proposed capital he selected a lovely stretch of land that lay in a Y shape formed by the Potomac River and its eastern branch, the Anacostia. This land was covered by marshes and woods. It had a few tobacco and other small farms. Several towns, including Georgetown in Maryland and Alexandria in Virginia, had developed in the region. Georgetown is now a well-to-do Washington neighborhood, and Alexandria is a suburb.

Europeans arrived on this land in the early 1600s. One of the first visitors—an English fur trapper named Henry Fleete—came in 1632. Soon, more Europeans settled and displaced the Native Americans. Thousands of Indians died of smallpox, a disease brought by the Europeans. As the colonies of Virginia and Maryland expanded to engulf what is now Washington, D.C., the settlers established farms and plantations, which were worked by African slaves.

Of course not everyone was satisfied with the decision to build the nation's capital in this backward, out-of-the-way spot. "A howling, malarious wilderness," grunted one official. "The Indian place . . . in the woods of the Potomac," said another. But George Wash-

Washington was founded in a wooded and marshy area between Maryland and Virginia.

The Earlier Inhabitants

For hundreds of years a Native American people called the Piscataway lived along the Potomac River in what is now Washington, D.C. The Piscataway grew corn and squash. Skilled craftspeople, they wove nets from reeds and caught fish in the rivers.

Waterbirds were also part of the Piscataway diet. Ducks were so thick on the Potomac River that Piscataway hunters brought them down with stones.■

The Potomac, Highway for the Ages

The Piscataway called their major river the *Patawomeke*, an Algonquin word meaning "trading place." Native Americans often took canoes up and down what we now know as the Potomac, trading goods as they went. The river continued to be an avenue of commerce when the Europeans arrived. In 1665, Georgetown was settled and became a river port. Alexandria was also a shipping center where huge bales of tobacco grown at nearby plantations were sent to distant markets. ■

Pierre Charles L'Enfant had a vision for Washington.

ington knew this area as well as anyone else in the nation. A man of vision, he saw future greatness here.

Congress called for the establishment of a 10-square-mile (26-sq-km) area to serve as a federal district for the capital city. Both Maryland and Virginia donated land to form that federal district, the original District of Columbia. Its boundaries were changed over the years, but to this day, the city of Washington lies entirely within the District of Columbia.

A Man and a Plan

On a June day in 1790, George Washington and Pierre Charles L'Enfant rode horses over the lonely lands along the Potomac. L'Enfant was a French engineer, artist, and architect. He was also an idealist who believed that a city's environment should excite the senses of its residents. He wrote to President Washington begging for a chance to create a capital "magnificent enough to grace a great nation." Washington was charmed by this Frenchman and his lofty dreams. The next year, the president appointed L'Enfant to be the project's chief engineer and planner. The two steered their horses up a prominent rise that was locally called Jenkins Hill. L'Enfant later wrote that this hill stood like "a pedestal waiting for a monument." Jenkins Hill soon got its monument.

The Capitol was erected on its peak and the rise is now known as Capitol Hill.

Even at its birth, the Federal City was a politically charged place. L'Enfant had an artistic temperament, and he clashed with politicians—and with landowners who influenced the politicians. It was L'Enfant's vision to create a city with broad boulevards that would radiate from the Capitol like spokes on a wheel. The architect also planned a "grand avenue four hundred feet in breadth" leading from the Capitol. Politicians and landowners complained that this layout was a waste of real estate. What was wrong with this mad Frenchman and his lust for wide avenues?

What's in a Word? The District of Columbia

In the eighteenth century, the United States was sometimes called Columbia, a name that derives from Christopher Columbus. Thus Congress called the land that held the infant capital the District of Columbia. Today, people call it the District, or simply D.C. ▪

George Washington inspecting the plans for the Capitol

Who Was Jenkins?

Why Capitol Hill was once called Jenkins Hill is a bit of a mystery. A family called Jenkins might have been tenant farmers there at one time, but there is no record that anyone named Jenkins ever owned the land where the magnificent U.S. Capitol stands today. ■

Few of his detractors realized that L'Enfant was inspired by Versailles, a breathtakingly beautiful city in France. Fewer still understood L'Enfant's desire to create an even grander metropolis than anything in Europe. L'Enfant realized the future greatness of the United States, and he was determined to build "a Federal City which is to become the Capital of this vast Empire."

The climax of L'Enfant's clash with his critics occurred over a house. A cousin of city commissioner and influential land baron Daniel Carroll built a large manor house that lay in the path of one

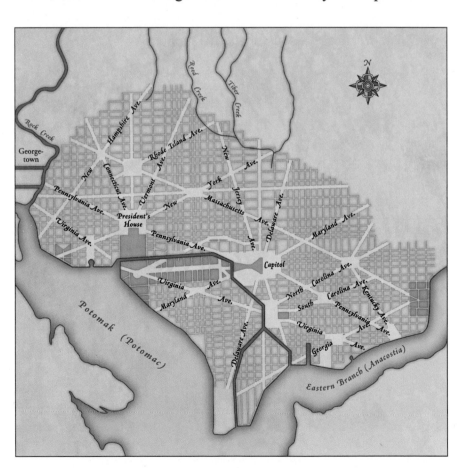

L'Enfant's plan for the Federal City

of L'Enfant's beloved boulevards. L'Enfant ordered workers to demolish the house. This was the final insult to the landowners and politicians. The crazy Frenchman had to go. After just a year on the job, L'Enfant was dismissed as the project's chief planner.

Daniel Carroll

But the plan drawn up by L'Enfant guided the future design of the city. His major road, which linked the Federal House (also called the Capitol) to the President's Palace (also known as the President's House and now called the White House), became Pennsylvania Avenue. The broad landscaped grounds leading from what is now Capitol Hill became the National Mall. Historians still argue about exactly how many of L'Enfant's ideas were used by future engineers, but all agree that, thanks to L'Enfant, the capital grew as a planned city. No other large city in the world had such an all-encompassing blueprint to shape its future.

Property Fight

The property owners of the Federal City were mainly farmers who had held the land for years. The federal government bought parcels of land, paying the owners in cash or giving them land in other parts of the proposed city. However, the farmers were not paid for their land that the architects had designated to become streets. Therefore the property owners were outraged by L'Enfant's plans to build a city with such wide avenues. ■

Broken Dreams, Broken Man

For his services, L'Enfant was offered $2,500 and a piece of land next door to the President's House (now known as the White House). He refused both the money and the land. L'Enfant reasoned that if the nation's leaders lacked the vision to share his ideas, then he should scorn their rewards. He died penniless in 1825. Eighty-four years later his remains were reburied on a commanding hill at Arlington National Cemetery. Visitors standing at L'Enfant's gravesite today (above) have a marvelous view of Washington, D.C, the city of his dreams.■

Work on the capital now fell to a competent and hardworking engineer named Andrew Ellicott. Wherever possible, Ellicott stayed true to the plans drawn up by Pierre L'Enfant. However, Ellicott had to work largely from memory because L'Enfant took most of his designs and drawings with him when he stormed off the job. Unlike his predecessor, Ellicott cooperated with the landowners and political leaders. Construction of the Federal City proceeded at a painfully slow but steady pace.

Ellicott was assisted by the remarkable Benjamin Banneker, who helped in reproducing the plans from memory. A free black farmer, Banneker had only a few months of formal schooling. Using borrowed books, he had taught himself astronomy and higher mathematics. He was at the time perhaps the most skilled surveyor in the country, and Ellicott chose him to lay out the city's streets. Banneker gave Washington an orderly grid of diagonal streets. Circles or squares later developed at intersections. The capital's streets today follow the pattern drawn up by Benjamin Banneker many years ago.

Andrew Ellicott had a better relationship with the landowners and political leaders than L'Enfant had.

Growing Pains

At first, the builders of the Federal City concentrated on two projects: the Federal House and the President's House. The buildings were 1.8 miles (2.5 km) from each other along the city's main street—now Pennsylvania Avenue.

Architects were invited to submit plans for the President's House, which was to have "true Elegance of proportion." The winner of this contest was Irish-born James Hoban. Construction

Banneker's Other Accomplishments

Just about anything in the physical or natural world interested Benjamin Banneker. He studied and wrote about the habits of bees and locusts. He built a remarkable clock out of raw wood, carving each gear by hand. The clock kept perfect time for more than fifty years. Banneker also published an almanac containing his observations on the movements of heavenly bodies. Though he was born free, his father was a slave. Banneker wrote many letters and essays calling for the abolition of slavery in the United States. ■

James Hoban's original design for the White House

began in 1792, making what we know today as the White House the oldest public building in Washington, D.C. Hoban modeled the structure after the large manor houses then popular in Britain and Ireland. Thomas Jefferson was later disappointed by the large size of the President's House, which he said was "big enough for two emperors, one Pope, and the grand lama."

In 1793, President George Washington laid the cornerstone of the Federal House. Once more a contest was announced and hopeful architects presented designs. The winner was William Thornton, a doctor and amateur architect. As a prize, Thornton was awarded $500 and a piece of land in Georgetown. His design called for a large building with two wings—one to serve as a meeting place for the Senate, the other for the House of Representatives. The two wings were to be connected by a wooden walkway and topped with a modest wooden dome. Thomas Jefferson, the architectural critic, approved of this design. He called the proposed building "simple, noble, beautiful."

Thomas Jefferson, Statesman and Architect

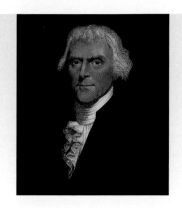

Thomas Jefferson served as secretary of state when the construction of Washington began. In 1801, he became the third president of the United States and the second president to live in the President's House. Jefferson was himself an accomplished architect who designed many buildings on his Virginia plantation called Monticello. Some historians believe Jefferson secretly submitted his own plans for the President's House under the assumed initials "A.Z.," but his designs were turned down. ■

These early government structures were built with the help of slave labor. Every morning, hundreds of slaves were marched to the building sites from neighboring farms and plantations. The federal government paid the slaves' owners for the slaves' services, but the slaves themselves received no wages. The owners were expected to provide slaves with sufficient food and clothing, nothing more. Most white residents at the time didn't pay attention to the terrible irony that the capital city of the "Land of the Free" was being built by slaves.

What's in a Word: the Capital and the Capitol

Washington is the capital (spelled with an *a*) of the United States, and in Washington stands the Capitol (spelled with an *o*)—the building where the Senate and the House of Representatives meet. These two different words cause many, many spelling errors. A *capital* is the center of government or activity of a nation. The word *capitol* stems from the temple of Jupiter that once stood on Capitoline Hill in Rome. That temple was used as a meeting place in ancient times. From its beginnings, the meetinghouse for the U.S. Congress was called the Capitol. And, to this day, the Capitol is the proud symbol of the nation's capital city. ■

The Old Stone House

The White House is the oldest public building in Washington, predating the Capitol by about a year. However, the oldest house still standing in the city is the Old Stone House in the Georgetown neighborhood. The Old Stone House, built by a cabinetmaker named Christopher Layman in 1764, is believed to be the only house in Washington that was constructed before the Revolutionary War. ■

Washington officially became the nation's capital in 1800. In November of that year, 126 clerks and officials, who made up practically the entire federal government payroll at the time, moved into town. Most were disappointed with what they saw. Pennsylvania Avenue was a muddy wagon trail. Only one wing of the Capitol was completed. Slave quarters and shacks put up by free workers stood everywhere. Oliver Wolcott, the secretary of the treasury, noted, "There are few houses in any one place, and most of them small miserable huts . . . . The people [in Washington] are poor, and as far as I can judge, they live like fishes, by eating each other."

President John Adams made the difficult eight-day wagon journey from Philadelphia—the temporary capital—to Washington. His family was

John Adams and his family were the first inhabitants of the White House.

the first to move into the President's House, which still smelled of wet cement. To enter the front door, Adams had to walk across a temporary plank bridge or risk sinking up to his knees in the mud outside. His wife, Abigail Adams, complained, "The house is habitable, but there is not a single apartment [room] finished." Still, John Adams entered the White House and offered a hopeful prayer: "I pray heaven to bestow the best of blessings on this house, and all that shall hereafter inhabit it. May none but honest and wise men ever rule under its roof."

The City of Washington

In 1801, the new capital was incorporated under the name the City of Washington. No longer was it called the Federal City. The capital's name officially honored President George Washington, who had died in 1799. ■

CHAPTER THREE

Nineteenth-Century Washington

The first half of the 1800s were turbulent years as war, regional quarrels, and the horrors of slavery brought suffering to the country and to its capital city. Yet Washington grew as the heart and soul of an ever-expanding nation. The second half of the 1800s saw the United States and Washington achieve greatness.

In the early 1880s, the roads in Washington remained unpaved.

War Comes to Washington

Early in its history, a French diplomat came to Washington, looked around at the shacks, the unfinished buildings, and the dirt roads, and cried out, "My God, what have I done to be condemned to reside in such a city?" Some European countries gave their diplomats extra "hardship pay" to compensate them for living in this backward capital. Roads were unpaved. Hotels and boardinghouses were crude. Members of Congress and foreign guests complained that the inns served food that was, at best, "uncivilized."

For decades after its birth, the capital had the look of a work in progress whose creators had grown tired in the middle of the job. The United States had very little money to spend on its capital city, and building materials and skilled workers were in short supply in this remote region. Work on the Capitol dragged on for years. Other public structures, such as the Treasury building, also suffered

Opposite: A view of the Washington Monument in 1884

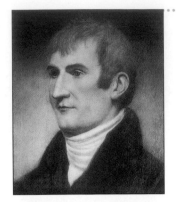

Meriwether Lewis

William Clark

frustrating delays. Washington was in desperate need of decent hotels, but few private investors were willing to spend money here. Investors feared the government would change its mind and transfer the nation's capital to some existing city.

Yet the business of state was carried on in a more or less ordinary fashion. In 1803, two young men, Meriwether Lewis and William Clark, dined with President Thomas Jefferson in the President's House. The two then ventured out on their famous 8,000-mile (12,800-km) expedition to the Pacific Ocean and back. A few months earlier, Jefferson had signed the Louisiana Purchase agreement, which doubled the size of the United States.

Despite its ramshackle appearance, early Washington was an exciting place because of the wide variety of people visiting there. Native Americans from the West came to negotiate with government leaders. Some chiefs wore flowing robes and war paint. The government treated the Indians with great dignity, even while officials drew up treaties that robbed them of the land they had lived

President James Buchanan with members of the Pawnee and Ponca tribes

Free Black Society

From the start, many free blacks settled in Washington. Free blacks had either been born to a free mother, purchased their freedom, or been given their freedom by a generous master. Free blacks often moved from slave states to the nation's capital. In 1830, some 12,000 African-Americans lived in Washington, and about half that number were free.

Free blacks in early Washington worked as shoemakers, cabinetmakers, plasterers, printers, and wagon drivers. The first school for free black children opened in 1807, and black churches were numerous.

Most free black workers lived in poverty, but several prospered. For example, Alfred Lee, a free black man, established a thriving store and grew rich enough to purchase a mansion that once housed the British Embassy. ■

on for hundreds of years. Strikingly dressed diplomats from far-away places such as Turkey and North Africa roamed the capital's streets alongside French envoys who wore the latest Paris fashions. And blacks were always present. About one-third of Washington's population in 1810 was made up of African-Americans.

In June 1812, the U.S. Congress met in Washington and voted to declare war on Great Britain. The nation's anger stemmed from Great Britain's continued presence in the American West. Furthermore, British warships frequently stopped U.S. vessels on the high seas. No one at the time realized how this war—the War of 1812—would affect the capital city.

On August 24, 1814, shouts and frightened cries rocked Washington's streets: "The

Sir George Cockburn asking the British troops for a vote on burning Washington during the War of 1812

British army is coming here. The enemy is upon us!" Five days earlier, the British had landed 4,000 troops at the town of Benedict, Maryland, some 40 miles (64 km) from the capital. At the nearby village of Bladensburg, the British troops routed a U.S. Army unit made up mostly of untrained farmboys. Now the red-coated soldiers, with gleaming bayonets pointing from their rifles, marched on Washington.

Residents of the capital raced about in a panic as they sought to escape. Poor people stuffed their few household goods into sacks and took to the roads carrying the sacks over their shoulders. Well-to-do men and women packed up their possessions in wagons. One such woman was Dolley Madison, wife of President James Madison. Rushing in and out of the President's House, Mrs. Madison loaded a wagon with valuable government papers and household goods. Carefully she placed in the wagon a stunning portrait of George Washington painted by the famous artist Gilbert Stuart. Then she joined the crowded roadways with thousands of others streaming out of the city.

Dolley Madison saved this now-famous portrait of George Washington painted by Gilbert Stuart.

The British army found the streets of Washington virtually deserted. A group of officers entered the President's House. Dolley Madison, knowing the British would break in, had not even bothered to lock the front door. The officers discovered food and wine still on the table and helped themselves to a hearty meal.

Dolley Madison's Heroics

Thanks to Dolley Madison, the Gilbert Stuart portrait of Washington hangs in the White House to this day. Saving the painting as the British army closed in was no easy task. Mrs. Madison discovered the frame was screwed to the wall, so she ordered servants to break the frame and remove the portrait. ■

As darkness closed in, the British troops went on a rampage, looting and burning buildings. The President's House and the Capitol were set on fire. The War and Treasury Department buildings were also burned. However, the British soldiers did not harm the few civilians who lingered in the city. And the troops did not wantonly set fire to private houses.

From a nearby hill, President James Madison and Attorney General Richard Rush looked down on a capital in flames. Rush wrote, "columns of flame and smoke ascended throughout the

The burning of Washington by the British

The ruins of the Capitol after the fire in 1814

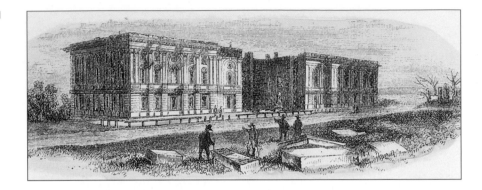

night. . . . The President's House and other public edifices were on fire, some burning slowly, others with bursts of flame and sparks mounting high up in the dark heavens."

A sudden rainstorm put out the fires. The next day the British army left the city. Slowly, Washingtonians returned. One resident looked at her city in ashes and gloomily wrote, "It is not expected that Washington will ever again be the seat of government."

Rebirth of the City

Instead of giving up, Washingtonians plunged into the job of rebuilding. The rebirth of the city was a slow process. It was five years before Congress met in the Capitol again. Restoring the President's House took three years. When the President's House was finished, workers put a fresh coat of white paint on the outside walls.

In the 1820s, new states west of the Appalachian Mountains developed. Politicians from those states tended to be rugged pioneers who enjoyed a rollicking good time at parties. When Andrew Jackson, from the frontier state of Tennessee, was inaugurated as president in 1829 his followers came to Washington to celebrate and

The Heroic Dr. Thornton

British soldiers entered the U.S. Patent Office where hundreds of plans for inventions and models of machinery were stored. They were about to burn the building when William Thornton, the architect who designed the Capitol, dashed up on horseback. Reportedly, he screamed at the officers in charge, "Are you Englishmen or are you vandals?" The officers, thus shamed, spared the Patent Office. ■

What's in a Name? The White House

Many historians point out that even before the War of 1812 the name White House was in use because the building had a white sandstone exterior, making it stand out among the many red brick buildings. In the nineteenth century, the White House was also called the Executive Mansion. Not until 1901, during the administration of President Theodore Roosevelt, did the words "White House" appear on the president's stationery. That made it official. ■

a near riot broke out. Crowds jammed the White House, tearing down curtains and breaking expensive dishes. President Jackson had to climb through a back window to escape his well-wishers.

In 1829, a wealthy British scientist named James Smithson died and left Washington an unusual gift. Smithson gave his enormous fortune to the United States to establish an institution whose mission was "the increase and diffusion of knowledge among men." Smithson had never even visited the United States. It is a mystery why Smithson gave this large sum of money to a country he had

A Look at the Smithsonian Today

In 1996, the Smithsonian Institution celebrated its 150th birthday. Fireworks and brass bands gathered on the Mall to honor the event. Over a century and a half, the Smithsonian empire has grown to include sixteen museums and galleries in Washington, two museums in New York City, the National Zoo in the capital, a sprawling wildlife preserve in the Blue Ridge Mountains, an astrophysics lab at Harvard University, and a research station in Panama. In its various facilities, the Smithsonian displays objects ranging from the bones of ancient Indians to rocks taken from the surface of the moon. Among its treasures are the bones of James Smithson, which were dug up from his grave in Italy and reinterred in the Smithsonian administration building. ■

never seen. He requested only that the establishment be called the Smithsonian Institution.

Smithson's money arrived in 105 bags containing some 100,000 gold coins. The gift was worth about $550,000, making it one of the largest single fortunes on Earth. Some congressmen argued that the United States should return the money because it was beneath the country's dignity to accept "charity." However the money was wisely used to establish the Smithsonian Institution in Washington. Today, the Smithsonian Institution is the largest museum complex in the world.

A colorful ceremony was held on July 4, 1848, as officials gathered to lay the cornerstone for the Washington Monument. The crowd sang "Yankee Doodle" as officials spread cement with the same trowel George Washington had used on the cornerstone of the Capitol more than fifty years earlier. After work began, funds for the Washington Monument project were exhausted. It took thirty-seven years to complete the marvelous obelisk that now stands almost as a badge of the capital city.

The first half of the nineteenth century saw the country expand from the Atlantic to the Pacific shores. Washington grew from a village of 14,000 people in 1800 to a small city of almost 40,000 by 1850. Yet the country and its capital were haunted by the specter of slavery. Thomas Jefferson said that slavery alarmed the people like "a firebell [ringing] in the night."

A House Divided

The Irish poet Thomas Moore visited early Washington and wrote these biting lines:

Even here beside the proud Potomac's streams . . .
The medley mass of pride and misery
Of whips and charters, manacles and rights
Of slaving blacks and democratic whites

Moore was one of many observers to point out that the unspeakably cruel system of slavery thrived in the capital city of

Slaves were bought and sold in markets like these in the capital city.

a land dedicated to liberty. In the early 1800s, it was common to see lines of slaves, sometimes chained together, being marched down Pennsylvania Avenue. A slave market operated near the Capitol. At the slave market, men and women were forced to stand naked while prospective buyers examined them as if they were cattle. Guests in Washington boardinghouses were allowed to chain their slaves in the basements while they strolled around the town. John Randolph, a Virginian and himself a slaveholder, called the slaves' condition in Washington, "a crying shame before God and man."

Many Washington slaves resisted the system by defying their masters with work slowdowns. Others attempted to escape, even though they knew that if captured they could be punished by whipping or by branding with a red-hot iron. The Washington area held several houses on the Underground Railroad, a secret organization that helped slaves to reach freedom. The runaway slave Harriet Tubman, one of the most courageous agents on the Underground Railroad, led escaping slaves down country roads outside of Washington. In 1848, about seventy Washington slaves secretly boarded a ship called the *Pearl* in the Potomac River and attempted to sail to freedom. Unfavorable winds thwarted the *Pearl*'s escape attempt.

By the late 1850s, the population of the United States approached 30 million people, including 4 million slaves. Slavery had faded in the Northern states, but it remained firm in the South. Arguments over slavery turned the nation into two camps—North and South, each hostile to the other. Washington, the capital, was a battleground between these two forces. Congressmen carried guns and knives to meetings, never knowing when they would have to defend themselves from bodily attack. At the Capitol in 1856, Representative Preston Brooks of South Carolina marched up to Charles Sumner, a senator from Massachusetts, and beat him over the head with a cane. Sumner spent more than two years recovering from his injuries. Brooks's Southern friends sent him new canes to replace the one he broke during the beating.

The Compromise of 1850

The buying and selling of slaves was made illegal in Washington, D.C., by the Compromise of 1850. That act of Congress was one of several compromise measures that lawmakers hoped would defuse the bitter arguments flaring up between Northern and Southern states. However, slavery itself remained legal in Washington until 1863. ◼

The Frederick Douglass National Historic Site

Frederick Douglass was one of the greatest antislavery spokesmen in the pre–Civil War era. Born a slave in Maryland, he escaped at age twenty-one. Once free, he founded an antislavery newspaper called the *North Star*. A fiery speaker, Douglass thrilled audiences as he denounced the evils of the slave system. In 1877, Douglass bought a pleasant house called Cedar Hill in Washington's Anacostia neighborhood. He spent the rest of his life there, working on behalf of African-American people. Today, the house is preserved as the Frederick Douglass National Historic Site, and visitors come to admire the work of this remarkable man. ◼

Abraham Lincoln was elected president in 1860.

"A house divided against itself cannot stand. I believe this government cannot endure permanently half slave and half free." These prophetic words were spoken in 1858 by a then little-known Illinois lawyer named Abraham Lincoln. In 1860, Lincoln was elected president. He had no plans to abolish slavery. Instead, he simply hoped the system would die a natural death. Still, he was hated in the South. When Lincoln came to Washington to celebrate his inauguration, many leaders feared his Southern enemies would assassinate him. Soldiers stood guard along the streets during Lincoln's inauguration parade. Sharpshooters were stationed on rooftops and ordered to gun down anyone who appeared ready to harm the new president. Five weeks after Lincoln's inauguration, Southern forces fired upon Fort Sumter, and the bloody American Civil War broke out.

The war raged for four years, from 1861 to 1865. Pitched battles were fought from Pennsylvania to Texas. On at least two occasions, the capital city was in danger of being captured by Southern armies. In July 1861, Southern forces defeated a Northern army at the Battle of Bull Run, just 30 miles (48 km) from the capital. In 1864, a battle was fought at Fort Stevens, about 4 miles (6.5 km) from the White House. During those battles, Washingtonians saw dead cavalry horses, and sometimes the broken bodies of soldiers, floating down the Potomac.

During the Civil War, Washington was a base camp for thousands of soldiers as well as a vast hospital for badly wounded and dying troops. Tent camps popped up in all the city's parks. Churches and private homes became makeshift hospitals. Even the Capitol served briefly as a hospital for wounded and sick soldiers.

Holmes's Heroics

When the fighting began at Fort Stevens, President Abraham Lincoln rode out to observe the battle firsthand. According to a famous story, the president, who was 6 feet 4 inches tall (193 cm), stood on the top of the fort's wall to get a better view. "Get down, you fool!" shouted a young officer. Lincoln ducked, and seconds later a volley of bullets whistled above him. Lincoln then said to the officer, "Young man, I'm glad you know how to talk to a civilian." The officer was Oliver Wendell Holmes (right), who later became one of the greatest justices ever to serve on the U.S. Supreme Court. ■

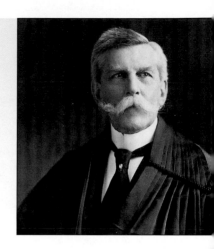

Escaped slaves swarmed into the city seeking refuge. In just four years, Washington's population doubled from 60,000 to 120,000. A Washington resident named Mary Clemmer Ames remembered that frantic time, "The endless roll of army wagons seemed never still. The rattle of the anguish-laden ambulance, the piercing cries of the sufferers whom it carried, made morning, noon, and night

Troops occupying the East Room of the White House during the Civil War

John Wilkes Booth shot Abraham Lincoln at Ford's Theatre in 1865.

Rebuilding the Capitol

Throughout the Civil War, hundreds of workers were engaged in a massive expansion of the Capitol. Two new wings and the huge dome were added. Many officials wanted work on the Capitol to halt because the project used resources desperately needed for the war effort. But President Lincoln insisted the expansion continue as a sign "we intend the Union shall go on." ■

too dreadful to be borne. . . . Every moment had its drum-beat, every hour was alive with the tramp of troops going, coming."

As the war increased in ferocity, about 2,000 wounded and sick soldiers were shipped to Washington hospitals each week. Many of the soldiers died, and the government looked about for a burial ground. Across the Potomac, in Arlington, Virginia, lay a large plantation owned by the Southern general Robert E. Lee. Northern leaders decided to bury dead soldiers on that plantation. Many historians say the North chose to convert the property into a cemetery in order to spite Robert E. Lee. By war's end, about 18,000 soldiers, from the South as well as the North, were buried there. The one-time plantation is now the Arlington National Cemetery, the most famous cemetery in the United States.

Just five days after the armies of the South surrendered, President Lincoln and his wife attended a play at Ford's Theatre in Washington. A Southern sympathizer named John Wilkes Booth sneaked up to the president's box with a pistol and shot Lincoln in the head. About nine hours later, the president died. A terrible sadness enveloped the city. For many U.S. citizens, it seemed that the death of their leader spelled the end of the world.

The Post–Civil War Years

It was called "democracy's greatest parade." Some 200,000 men plus hundreds of horse-drawn artillery pieces passed in review down Pennsylvania Avenue to mark the end of the Civil War. But only the first few rows of spectators could see the marching troops. The others saw only a cloud of dust that hovered over the soldiers' heads. Like most of Washington's streets at that time, Pennsylvania Avenue, the capital's main street, was still unpaved. The city also lacked sidewalks and, worst of all, sewers. Flooding after summer rainstorms covered the capital in a lake of muck and mud.

Washington needed a leader—a top boss—who would do the tough work of improving the city's infrastructure. The capital got such a boss in Alexander Shepherd. Born in poverty, Shepherd became rich by operating Washington's most successful plumbing business. In 1870, Shepherd was appointed vice president of the city's Board of Public Works. He launched a program that provided 120 miles (193 km) of sewers, 208 miles (335 km) of sidewalks, 150 miles (241 km) of road improvements, and 30 miles (48 km) of water mains. Also, under Shepherd's direction, more than 60,000 trees were planted along the city streets. He was called Boss

Ford's Theatre Today

Shortly after President Lincoln's assassination, the federal government bought Ford's Theatre and installed offices in the building. In the 1960s, the theater was restored to resemble the way it had looked 100 years earlier. Visitors today see Box Seven, where Lincoln was sitting the night he was shot. On display are the murder weapon and the flag that covered Lincoln's coffin. Across the street is the restored Petersen House, where Lincoln died at 7:22 A.M. on April 15, 1865. Doctors had moved Lincoln to the Petersen House because they believed his head wound was so severe he would not survive a trip to the White House. ■

Shepherd, and he often acted as if his wishes were law. For example, when a railroad company refused to relocate its tracks, Shepherd sent a crew to tear the tracks from the ground.

Immediately after the Civil War about 30 percent of Washington's people were black, many of them newly freed slaves. Congress established the Freedmen's Bureau in 1865 to create education and job programs for African-Americans. Two years later, the Freedmen's Bureau helped found Howard University in Washington. To this day, Howard University is hailed as a distinguished predominantly black college. Though the majority of the city's black people were poor, they established a dynamic community in the capital. Two African-American newspapers, the *Washington Bee* and *Colored American*, enjoyed wide readership. An all-black opera company gave regular performances. Debates and discussions attracted overflow audiences at the Bethel Literary Society, a black cultural group.

"Washington is rapidly becoming a city worthy of [being] the nation's capital," said President Ulysses S. Grant shortly after the Civil War. Elegant mansions rose along the avenues, and modern hotels replaced the shabby boardinghouses that were once prevalent. The government contributed to this building boom with the addition of the State, War, and Navy building in 1888 and the Library of Congress in 1897.

In 1885, the Washington Monument was finally completed. Rising more than 555 feet (169 m) into the sky, it was then the tallest structure in the world. The Smithsonian Institution's Arts and Industries building was completed in 1880. In the 1890s, land was set aside for Rock Creek Park, one of the finest city parks in the

nation today. Washington began to look more and more like L'Enfant's dream—a magnificent city laced with elegant boulevards.

In December 1900, Washington celebrated its 100th birthday as the seat of government for the United States. The twentieth century would be called the American Century because in that 100-year span the United States became the world's mightiest and most influential nation. And, throughout this crucial American Century, Washington was the heart of that nation.

The State, War, and Navy building was built in 1888.

CHAPTER FOUR

Washington and the American Century

J acob S. Coxey, a tough scrap-iron dealer from Ohio, put out a call for 100,000 unemployed men to march with him to Washington and carry their grievances to the nation's leaders. "Coxey's Army" began its march in 1894, a time of economic depression, but only about 500 jobless men actually joined the so-called army. Once the men were in the city, police arrested Jacob Coxey for walking on the lawn at Capitol Hill. In many ways, the ill-fated Coxey's Army was the opening act of a continuing Washington drama. Throughout the 1900s, the capital was the focal point for protests as well as celebrations. No other city reflected the nation's good times as well as its tragedies as did the capital.

Coxey's Army marched into Washington in 1894, marking the first demonstration in the nation's capital.

Progress and Depression

In the early twentieth century, railroad travel reached its zenith. Fittingly, Washington's spectacular Union Station opened in 1907. The huge terminal—longer than two football fields—was the biggest train depot in the country. The new Union Station allowed city planners to tear down an unsightly depot and to eliminate a set of railroad tracks that crossed the city. This done, planners concentrated on making the National Mall the showcase it is today. When it was

Opposite: Taking in the wonder of the Lincoln Memorial

completed, the Mall ran from the Capitol to the Potomac River. Marshland was drained near the riverbank to create parks. Designers drew up plans to build a stately memorial to Abraham Lincoln at the Potomac end of the Mall.

In 1917, the United States joined World War I, the terrible conflict that had been raging in Europe for three years. The capital city always becomes more important during a war. In two years, Washington's population swelled from 350,000 to 450,000 people. The war ended in 1918, and once more a triumphant parade was held on Pennsylvania Avenue. World War I was called "the war to end all wars."

The Lincoln Memorial was dedicated in 1922. The seated statue of Lincoln brooding over the Reflecting Pool became one of the most breathtaking sights in Washington. Several prominent black leaders were honored guests at the dedication ceremony. However, the blacks had to sit in a roped-off section. Washington, D.C., is in the southern United States, where racial segregation was then the law of the land. Even at an event honoring Abraham Lincoln, the "Great Emancipator," African-Americans were treated as a people apart.

The 1920s were a boom decade in the United States. The stock market reached dizzying new highs, providing wealth and jobs for millions. Then, in the fall of 1929, the collapse of the stock market ushered in the Great Depression of the 1930s. Desperate Americans took their frustrations to Washington. In the summer of 1932, thousands of "bonus marchers" arrived in the capital. The marchers were World War I veterans who demanded that Congress give them bonus money for their service in the armed forces. Congress refused. An ugly riot broke out as army troops evicted the bonus marchers from huts they had built on the Anacostia flats.

Franklin D. Roosevelt was sworn in as president in 1933, perhaps the worst year of the Great Depression. He tried to calm the nation in his inaugural address by saying, "The only thing we have to fear is fear itself." The president launched a program called the New Deal, which was designed to give work to the jobless. A small army of administrators, called New Dealers, moved into the city. Many New Dealers settled in Georgetown and launched that neighborhood's revitalization.

President Franklin D. Roosevelt led the country during the Great Depression.

Washington's African-American residents suffered unemployment as well as the day-to-day humiliation of living in a segregated city. In 1939, Marian Anderson, the world's greatest contralto, attempted to give a concert in Washington's Constitution Hall. But a women's organization called the Daughters of the American Revolution (DAR) refused to let her perform in Constitutional Hall because she was black. The refusal infuriated Eleanor Roosevelt, the wife of the president and herself a DAR member. With Eleanor Roosevelt's help, Anderson gave a concert in front of the Lincoln Memorial. Some 75,000 people attended. Many in the audience wept when Anderson sang the spiritual, "Nobody Knows the Trouble I've Seen."

Contralto Marian Anderson gave a moving concert in front of the Lincoln Memorial in 1939.

President Roosevelt's funeral procession

World War II and the Postwar Years

"Yesterday, December 7, 1941—a date which will live in infamy—the United States of America was suddenly and deliberately attacked by naval and air forces of the Empire of Japan." So said President Roosevelt to a joint session of Congress after Japan's sneak air attack on the U.S. naval base at Pearl Harbor, Hawaii. Roosevelt asked for and received a declaration of war.

United States forces fought in World War II from December 1941 to August 1945. Washington, the command city, buzzed with activity. Soldiers, sailors, diplomats from foreign countries, and hordes of office workers swarmed into town. The Pentagon, which sits on the Virginia shore across from Washington and ranks as the world's largest office building, was completed in 1943 to house the War Department. The enormous Pentagon building was soon the daytime home of more than 30,000 office workers.

In April 1945, as World War II drew to a close, the nation was saddened by President Roosevelt's death. Men and women cried openly as Roosevelt's funeral procession wound down Pennsylvania Avenue.

The 1950 census counted 802,178 Washington residents. The city's population would go no higher. In the postwar years, Washingtonians began leaving the city for neat and tidy homes in the suburbs. A desire for space and greenery was one reason for the suburban migration. Race was another factor. The vast majority of residents who moved to the suburbs were white. Most suburbs were closed to blacks. By the mid-1950s, African-Americans were in the majority in Washington, making it the first major U.S. city where blacks made up more than half the population. The suburbs, on the other hand, were almost entirely white.

In the years to come, the population of the city of Washington continued to decline while the suburbs mushroomed. Most suburbanites were government workers who commuted to and from the city. The federal government joined the suburban trend by building the National Institutes of Health in Bethesda, Maryland, and the Central Intelligence Agency in McLean, Virginia.

The Off-Color White House

When the United States became involved in World War II, military officers feared that enemy bombers would raid East Coast cities, including Washington. Several generals suggested that the White House be painted a different color—perhaps green or black—to confuse the bombers. President Roosevelt refused to consider the paint job. ■

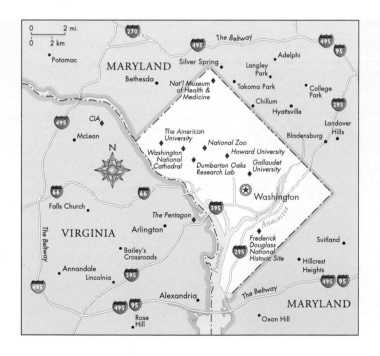

The Beltway

Washington's suburbs are strung together by Interstate 495, which is generally called the Beltway. The Beltway forms a circle about 12 miles (19 km) in diameter around the city and its major suburbs. Newspaper and TV reporters often talk about life "inside the Beltway," meaning the vast community of the greater Washington area inside Interstate 495. ■

Washington's suburbs and interstates

Free World Capital and a Troubled City

After World War II, much of the world looked to the United States for leadership. However, the nation's capital city was becoming increasingly impoverished and plagued with crime. Still, Washington remained the center of attention for U.S. and Free World residents. In many ways, the city was a theater expressing the drama of the times.

On a crisp January morning in 1961, President John F. Kennedy took his oath of office on the steps of the Capitol. Kennedy was youthful and witty with movie-star good looks. The country also adored his wife and two small children. Then, on November 22, 1963, came the shocking, unbelievable word that John F. Kennedy had been shot and killed in Dallas, Texas. His body was flown back to Washington, to lie in state at the Capitol's Rotunda. Lines of mourners forty blocks long waited to pay their respects to the fallen president. No one alive at the time will forget the dignity displayed by Jacqueline Kennedy as she walked behind the horse-drawn casket in her husband's funeral procession.

In late August 1963, more than 200,000 people descended on the National Mall to hear Martin Luther King Jr. give his dramatic speech: "I have a dream that one day this nation will rise up and live out the true meaning of its creed: 'We hold

President Kennedy's coffin being carried up the stairs of the Capitol

Martin Luther King Jr. addressing the crowd during the March on Washington in 1963

these truths to be self-evident; that all men are created equal.'" The speech was part of the March on Washington to demand equal rights for African-Americans. Some leaders feared the event would explode into bloody fighting. Instead, the march was a celebration that saw blacks and whites holding hands and singing songs of freedom. More than four years later, King was assassinated in Memphis, Tennessee, and riots broke out in scores of U.S. cities. Some of the worst rioting took place in Washington, D.C., where ten people were killed and National Guard troops were called in to restore order. No Washingtonian will forget the sight of machine guns set up on Pennsylvania Avenue.

For the United States, the 1960s was a decade of change, frustration, and violence. The Vietnam War dragged on, and at its peak took more than 100 U.S. young lives each week. In 1967, a huge antiwar protest called the March on the Pentagon began at the National Mall and proceeded to the Pentagon building. Two years

Sides squaring off during the anti–Vietnam War protest at the Pentagon in 1967

later, about 1,000 poor people set up tents and shacks on the Mall and proclaimed their settlement "Resurrection City." The Resurrection City dwellers said they would remain on the Mall until the government provided help for impoverished people, but their movement lost steam after a few weeks.

Drug addiction became a scourge in the Washington slums in the 1970s and 1980s. Drugs breed crime, and year after year the murder statistics soared. Many journalists called Washington the "murder capital of the United States." The city's high crime rate and failing school system increased the movement to the suburbs. Housing discrimination in the outlying communities ended, and middle-class black families joined the suburban flight. By the late 1990s, the population of greater Washington (including its suburbs) had grown to more than 4 million people, while Washington proper (within the city limits) had diminished to just more than 500,000.

The National Mall has remained the country's gathering point for protestors. The Mall is a magnet for demonstrations because of its sheer size and the fact that the long leafy park serves as the nation's nerve center. On several occasions the Mall was covered with a patchwork of 40,000 individual quilts to remind U.S. residents of the scourge of AIDS. In 1995, the Nation of Islam leader Louis Farrakhan brought hundreds of thousands of black men to the Mall to take part in the Million Man March. About a year later, a coalition of Christian groups called the Promise Keepers staged a mass rally on the Mall.

The AIDS quilt on display at the National Mall in 1992

Washington, despite its problems, remains a popular place to visit. By the 1990s, almost 20 million tourists a year crowded into the city. Its monuments, the Smithsonian and other museums, and its overpowering sense of history continue to delight visitors.

CHAPTER FIVE

The Capital's Natural Wonders

Many Washingtonians say that springtime, when the cherry trees bloom, is the best time to visit their city. Other residents recommend visiting in the fall when blazing autumn colors dazzle people walking in Rock Creek Park. Whatever the season, Washington is a gorgeous city and its stunning beauty is largely a gift of nature.

The Potomac River provides a picturesque setting for the capital.

The River Setting

Back in 1790, Congress asked George Washington to select a site along the Potomac River for the country's new capital. The heart of Washington remains along the riverbank, but the city limits now cover 68 square miles (177 sq km). The metropolitan area (including the suburbs) has spread out to engulf more than 6,500 square miles (16,835 km) in Maryland and Virginia.

Its rivers still mark the borders of Washington, D.C. The historic areas of the city are tucked between the Potomac River and its branch, the Anacostia. Rock Creek runs the width of the city, and Rock Creek Park is a popular playground. West Potomac and East Potomac Parks were made from reclaimed marshland along the Potomac. The two riverside parks now sprawl over 720 acres (291 ha) and hold many of the city's most famous monuments.

Opposite: The Jefferson Memorial with cherry blossoms in the foreground

Under the Arlington Bridge, which connects Arlington to Washington, D.C.

Near the riverbanks, Washington's land lies almost exactly at sea level. Beyond the two rivers rise several gentle hills. Capitol Hill, the most politically important hill in the world, is 88 feet (27 m) above sea level. Washington's highest point is a hill in the Tenleytown district that stands 410 feet (125 m) above sea level.

To the west, the Potomac forms Washington's boundary with the state of Virginia. The city's near suburb— Arlington, Virginia—has many historic attractions, including Arlington National Cemetery and the Iwo Jima statue. Arlington and Washington are connected by the lovely Arlington Memorial Bridge. The city borders the state of Maryland on the north, east, and south.

Plants and City Wildlife

Some 200 years ago, Washington's original trees were chopped down and carried away. The destruction of the trees alarmed one of the city's early residents—President Thomas Jefferson. The president worked to save the old trees remaining in the Mall area, and he planted rows of poplars along Pennsylvania Avenue. Jefferson, a farmer and a student of nature, was perhaps the first city leader to plant trees in the capital. Many more tree-planting efforts followed. In 1815, English elms replaced Jefferson's poplars on Pennsylvania Avenue, and those were eventually replaced by lindens, maples, oaks, and sycamores.

Today, about 1,800 varieties of plants and 250 different types of shrubs and trees grow in Washington. Many tree-lined streets are virtual caves of arching branches. The city's mild climate and ample rainfall encourage swift tree growth. In just a few years, trees sprout out of inner-city vacant lots and grow taller than surrounding houses. Common trees include black walnut, oak, sycamore,

The U.S. National Arboretum

For a special treat, plant lovers visit the U.S. National Arboretum, a 444-acre (180-ha) hillside park on the northeastern edge of the city. In this government-owned park, one of the largest arboretums in the country, rolling hills are covered with wildflowers, flowering trees, and shrubs. Azaleas, rhododendrons, and dogwoods explode in the colors of the season to the delight of visitors. ■

Rock Creek Park

One of the best places to enjoy nature in Washington is at Rock Creek Park, a 6-mile (10-km) long, 1,800-acre (728-ha) island of greenery. The park has more than 15 miles (24 km) of hiking trails and paths, many of which wind by the gently flowing Rock Creek. It also has an amazing variety of plants, wildflowers, and trees. Keep a sharp eye open and you may spot deer or an occasional fox. ■

magnolia, and dogwood. Oriental ginkgoes and Asiatic magnolias are among the exotic trees that came from other lands. Of course, Washington's most celebrated trees are the Japanese cherry trees that line the Potomac and the Tidal Basin. In the spring, blossoms cover the cherry trees with a coating of white that looks like pure snow.

Some 150 parks of various sizes dot the city. In the parks are wildfowers and plants such as jack-in-the-pulpits, Virginia bluebells, and golden groundsels. City gardeners grow roses, peonies, irises, and lilies. Many families raise tomatoes, sweet corn, green peppers, cucumbers, and grapes in their backyards.

Many kinds of flowers and other plants adorn the city sidewalks.

Eager Beavers

In spring 1999, some odd marks were found on cherry trees near the capital's tidal basin. Experts concluded the marks were made by gnawing teeth of beavers. For city officials this was a mixed blessing. First, it meant that the Potomac and the Anacostia Rivers were cleaner than in the past, when the waters were too polluted to support beaver life. But now the beavers—as beavers do—were chewing up the cherry trees that have long been the pride of Washington. Traps were set, and a family of three beavers was captured. The family was moved to a river system in a deep woods where, it is hoped, the beavers lived happily ever after. ■

A squirrel on the White House lawn

With Washington's abundance of trees, squirrels are found everywhere. Other city wildlife includes rabbits, raccoons, skunks, deer, foxes, and chipmunks. And, even though Washington is an inland city, it is home to flocks of seagulls. Pigeons are also numerous, much to the annoyance of the workers who clean the statues.

Washington's Geographical Features

Total area; rank	68 sq. mi. (177 sq km); 51st
Land area; rank	61 sq. mi. (158 sq km); 51st
Water area; rank	7 sq. mi. (18 sq km); 51st
Inland water; **rank**	7 sq. mi. (18 sq km); 51st
Geographic center	Near Fourth and L Streets Northwest
Highest point	Tenleytown at the Reno Reservoir, 410 feet (125 m) above sea level
Lowest point	Potomac River, 1 foot (30 cm) above sea level
Population; rank	606,900 (1990 census); 49th
Record high temperature	106°F (73°C) on July 20, 1930
Record low temperature	−15°F (−26°C) on February 11, 1988
Average July temperature	78°F (26°C)
Average January temperature	37°F (3°C)
Average annual precipitation	50 inches (127 cm)

Drenched Inaugural

A cold, miserable rain fell on Washington in March 1841. But the weather did not discourage newly elected President William Henry Harrison from participating in his inaugural parade. Harrison, who was once an army commander, rode triumphantly down Pennsylvania Avenue on a white horse. The president caught pneumonia and died thirty days later. ■

In the spring, warblers, thrushes, finches, and other songbirds come home to Washington. Bass, shad, sunfish, and catfish swim in the waters of the Potomac and its branches.

Climate

Washington enjoys a generally mild climate, but many city dwellers complain about its hot and sultry summers. The city was partially built over marshlands and suffers high humidity. Air conditioning on summer nights is recommended for sound sleep. Temperaturewise, winters in Washington are warmer than those in New York, Philadelphia, or even in the southern city of Memphis, Tennessee, but sudden blizzards and cold snaps can disrupt the capital.

The city's average January temperature is 37°F (3°C), and its average temperature in July is 78°F (26°C). When visiting Washington, be prepared for the possibility of extreme weather shifts. The record low was reached in February 1988 when the temperature dipped to –15°F (–26°C); the all-time high was 106°F (73°C), recorded in July 1930.

Washington averages 50 inches (127 cm) of total precipitation (rain or snow) each year. Because winters tend to be mild, yearly snowfall amounts to only about 17 inches (43 cm). When heavy snows do fall, Washington's usually snarling traffic jams become ferocious because the city lacks the equipment to clear the streets.

Snow in Washington can bring work and traffic to a standstill.

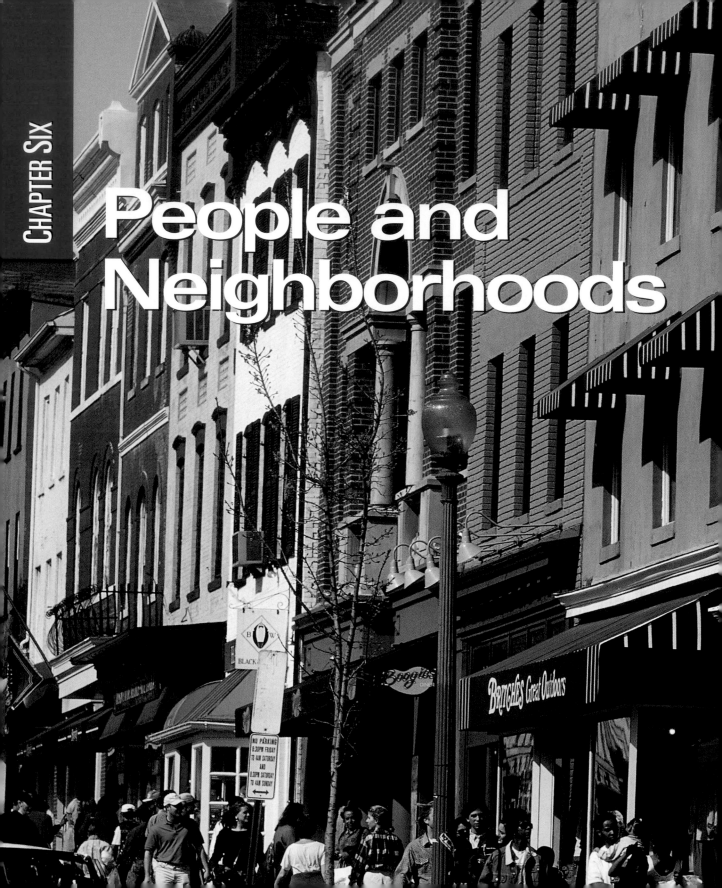

CHAPTER SIX

People and Neighborhoods

To casual observers, Washington may look like a city of tourists. Guests flock here from every country in the world to see the sights of the city. But some 4 million people live permanently in the Washington area. Like residents in other communities, Washingtonians work, go to church, and strive to make their neighborhood a better place to live.

Columbia, Maryland, is one of Washington's suburbs.

A Look at the People

Only about one-eighth of the people who call themselves Washingtonians actually live in the city. The capital's metropolitan area includes six counties in Maryland and five counties in Virginia. Counting its suburbs, the Washington region's 4 million people make it the eighth-largest metropolitan area in the nation. In contrast, the population within the city limits totals less than 610,000, ranking it nineteenth among U.S. cities.

Why has the city not grown as quickly as the suburbs? Many experts say it simply followed a national trend. Since World War II, other U.S. cities also declined in growth while their suburbs increased. Failing school systems and fear of crime are among the reasons cited for suburban flight. A 1995 study said that 22.2 percent of Washingtonians live below the poverty level. This figure is

Opposite: Shops on a Georgetown street

Shrinking Washington

Census figures taken during the twentieth century reflect the rise and decline of Washington's population. In 1998, the estimated population of the city (not including the suburbs) stood at about 550,000 people, down one-fourth since 1970.

1900	278,718
1920	437,571
1940	663,091
1950	802,178
1960	763,956
1970	756,510
1980	638,333
1990	606,900

Planned Suburbs

Most of the capital's suburbs grew in a more or less haphazard manner after World War II. As residents moved in, new houses were built and streets were laid out. But two suburbs—Columbia, Maryland, and Reston, Virginia (above)—were layed out by urban planners before they were built. Both suburbs began in the 1960s and are hailed today as models of city planning. Columbia is famed for its walkability. Its residents do not need a car to shop or go about other daily chores. ■

almost twice the national average. Many middle-class families, black and white, fled to the suburbs to escape the problems associated with poverty.

Certainly there are stable, prosperous neighborhoods in the city of Washington. Georgetown, for example, has fashionable shops and trendy restaurants. The major factors limiting Georgetown's population growth are its high rents and property prices. The Dupont Circle neighborhood, many areas downtown, and the Rock Creek Park vicinity are also very elegant places to live.

Most Washingtonians who live in the city proper rent rather than own their homes. About half the people live in two- and three-family dwellings. Only 36 percent of Washington's families are homeowners, while nationally 48 percent of city dwellers own their own homes. Washington has many luxurious high-rise apartment buildings, but good housing is very costly in the city. The desire to own an affordable home is another reason why families move to the suburbs.

Washington's Burgeoning Suburbs

How fast are Washington's suburbs growing? In terms of population, the suburb of Silver Spring is the second-largest town in the state of Maryland, and suburban Arlington (above) is the fourth-largest town in Virginia. ∎

The Watergate

One of the city's most prestigious addresses is the Watergate apartment complex. Called "a city within a city," the gracefully curving building has shops, restaurants, and expensive apartments. However, it has been connected with scandal. In 1972, burglars broke into the Democratic Party's headquarters in the Watergate. The burglars were suspected to be agents of the Republican Party, and the cover-up that followed the break-in led to the resignation of Republican president Richard Nixon. ∎

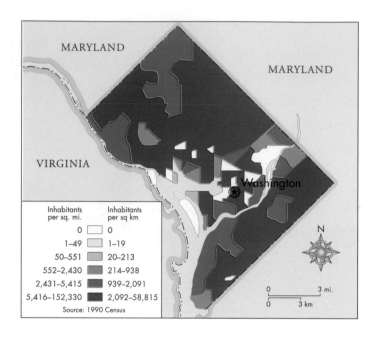

African-Americans are by far the majority group in the city, followed by whites, Hispanics, and Asians. About 41,000 people living in Washington are citizens of other countries. Many work for foreign embassies. Many residents have moved to the capital area in recent years from other states. Surveys show that only 40 percent of Washingtonians were actually born in the city.

Washington's population density

Black Washington, Success and Frustration

The population of Washington is about 66 percent black. Only the cities of Atlanta, Georgia, and Detroit, Michigan, have a larger percentage of African-American residents. The black presence in Washington has been prominent since its beginnings. Over the years blacks have thrived in the nation's capital, and they have also suffered frustration.

Edward Brooke grew up in Washington in the 1930s. A member of a middle-class black family, Brooke lived in a "quiet and friendly neighborhood [where] everyone knew just about everyone else." Brooke attended Washington's Dunbar High School and the prestigious Howard University. He later moved to Massachusetts, where he was elected to the U.S. Senate. Brooke witnessed the riots following the assassination of Martin Luther King Jr. "When rioting broke out in the city in 1968, I felt a special twinge of despair because the violence and disorder were taking place not far from the old neighborhood I had known and loved. And although I could not condone the violent activity that was rending the community, I could well understand the kinds of feelings and circumstances that had caused it."

The frustration Brooke referred to stemmed from poverty. The unemployment rate in Washington is far greater for blacks than for whites. In poor neighborhoods, the death rate for infants is twice the national average. The capital's public high schools are almost

Massachusetts senator Edward Brooke grew up in Washington.

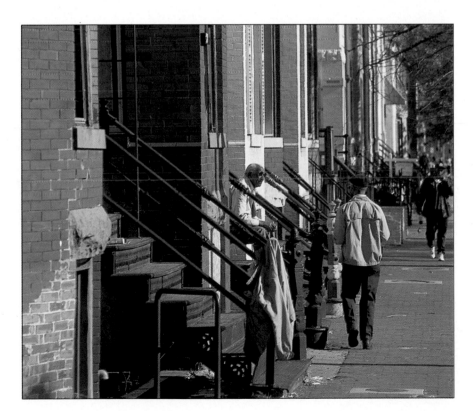

An African-American neighborhood

Ethnic distribution of Washington D.C. (Does not equal 100%)	
Black	66%
White	32%
Hispanic	6%
Asian	3%
Native American	0.2%

90 percent black, and four out of every ten students drop out before graduation. Critics claim there are two different cities operating in Washington: one is the capital of the world's richest nation; the other is the black community, where standards of living approach those of a Third World country.

Despite this grim picture, Washington is a success story for thousands of African-Americans. In 1997, the median income of black families in Washington was $39,896, the highest in the nation. The same 1997 study ranked Washington first in black

Dunbar High School, Home to Scholars

In the era when school systems were segregated, Washington's Dunbar High School was the finest black high school in the United States. Its graduates included Edward Brooke, the first African-American U.S. senator elected since the 1860s; Benjamin Davis, the first African-American general in the U. S. Army; and Charles Drew, a black physician known for his research on plasma and for setting up blood banks. ∎

Georgetown University was founded in 1789.

residents with a college degree and first in black families earning more than $75,000 a year. Many African-American leaders say Washington has a more vibrant black middle class than any other city in the nation.

Education

Washington public schools serve some 79,000 students, who attend classes in 186 school buildings. Until the mid-1950s, schools in the city were segregated—the city maintained separate school systems for white and black students. In many respects, the public schools are still segregated, not by law but by custom. Most white children and many middle-class blacks attend private schools. The city's private schools have about 10,000 students, of which about 4,800 students attended Catholic schools in the early 1990s.

Howard University

Opposite: Washington's neighborhoods

As of 1995, the city of Washington spent about $9,300 a year on each public school student, a figure that is well above the national average. Despite this generous budget, the school system is in deep trouble. Approximately 65 percent of the students test below their grade level, and the high school dropout rate is one of the worst in the nation. A 1997 report concluded, "In virtually every category and for every grade level [Washington's] public schools have failed to provide a quality education for all children."

While public grade and high schools need improvement, higher education flourishes in the capital. Washington is home to seventeen degree-granting colleges and universities. Georgetown University, founded in 1789, is the nation's oldest Catholic college. Today, Georgetown has almost 12,000 students. George Washington University, founded in 1821, is the capital's biggest college, with an enrollment approaching 20,000. American University (1893) serves 12,000 students. Howard University

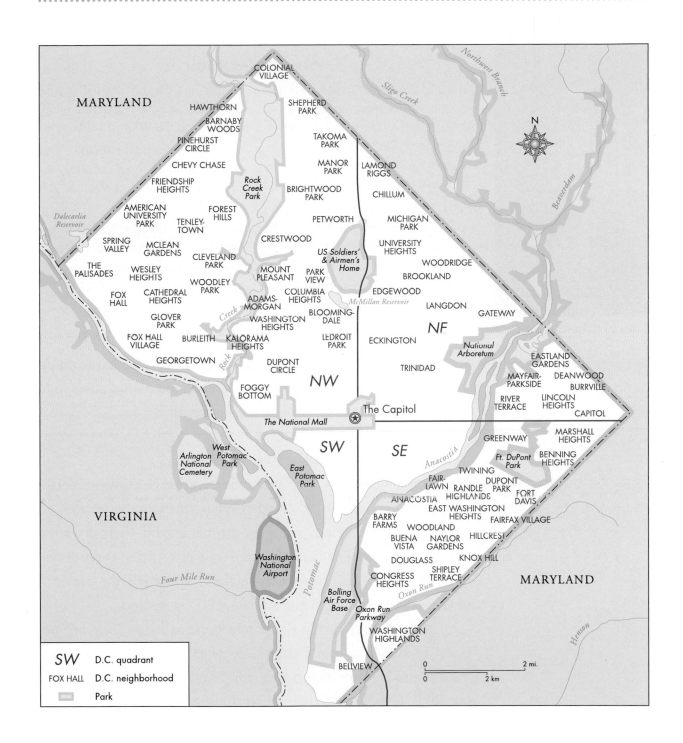

MARYLAND

COLONIAL
VILLAGE

HAWTHORN

BARNABY
WOODS

PINEHURST
CIRCLE

CHEVY CHASE

FRIENDSHIP
HEIGHTS

AMERICAN
UNIVERSITY
PARK

SPRING
VALLEY

THE
PALISADES

FOX
HALL

GLOVER
PARK

FOX HALL
VILLAGE

GEORGETOWN

FOREST
HILLS

TENLEY-
TOWN

MCLEAN
GARDENS

WESLEY
HEIGHTS

CATHEDRAL
HEIGHTS

BURLEITH

Rock
Creek
Park

CLEVELAND
PARK

WOODLEY
PARK

ADAMS-
MORGAN

Rock Creek

WASHINGTON
HEIGHTS

KALORAMA
HEIGHTS

SHEPHERD
PARK

TAKOMA
PARK

MANOR
PARK

BRIGHTWOOD
PARK

PETWORTH

CRESTWOOD

MOUNT
PLEASANT

PARK
VIEW

COLUMBIA
HEIGHTS

US Soldiers'
& Airmen's
Home

BLOOMING-
DALE

LEDROIT
PARK

Sligo Creek

Northwest Branch

LAMOND
RIGGS

CHILLUM

MICHIGAN
PARK

UNIVERSITY
HEIGHTS

WOODRIDGE

BROOKLAND

EDGEWOOD

McMillan Reservoir

LANGDON

ECKINGTON

Beaverdam

GATEWAY

NE

N

Dalecarlia
Reservoir

DUPONT
CIRCLE

FOGGY
BOTTOM

NW

TRINIDAD

National
Arboretum

EASTLAND
GARDENS

MAYFAIR-
PARKSIDE

DEANWOOD

BURRVILLE

RIVER
TERRACE

LINCOLN
HEIGHTS

CAPITOL

The Capitol

The National Mall

VIRGINIA

Arlington
National
Cemetery

West
Potomac
Park

East
Potomac
Park

SW

SE

Anacostia

GREENWAY

Ft. DuPont
Park

MARSHALL
HEIGHTS

BENNING
HEIGHTS

TWINING

FAIR-
LAWN

DUPONT
PARK

RANDLE
HIGHLANDS

FORT
DAVIS

ANACOSTIA

EAST WASHINGTON
HEIGHTS

FAIRFAX VILLAGE

Washington
National
Airport

Four Mile Run

Potomac

Bolling
Air Force
Base

Oxon Run
Parkway

BARRY
FARMS

WOODLAND

BUENA
VISTA

NAYLOR
GARDENS

DOUGLASS

HILLCREST

KNOX HILL

CONGRESS
HEIGHTS

SHIPLEY
TERRACE

Oxon Run

WASHINGTON
HIGHLANDS

MARYLAND

Henson

BELLVIEW

0   2 mi.

0   2 km

SW   D.C. quadrant

FOX HALL   D.C. neighborhood

       Park

The Willard Hotel

Many of the city's finest hotels are in the Northwest section. The Willard Hotel, less than two blocks from the White House, is a Washington fixture. The Willard has a long and interesting history:

The hotel dates back to the 1850s, and ten different presidents have stayed there.

The term *lobbyist*, meaning a person who tries to influence politicians, was coined there because influence peddlers enjoyed hanging around the Willard's lobby.

Julia Ward Howe wrote "The Battle Hymn of the Republic," the famous Civil War song, at the Willard.

Abraham Lincoln stayed at the Willard for a few days in 1861 and paid $4 a night for his room. Today, many rooms at the Willard cost more than $400 a night. ■

(1867) remains the best-known mostly black college in the country. Gallaudet University (1857) is a unique institution devoted to educating students who are hearing impaired.

The Capital's Neighborhoods

Washington is divided into four sections called Northwest, Northeast, Southeast, and Southwest. Boundary lines for the sections all intersect at the Capitol, and they are named for their direction from Capitol Hill. For example, the Northwest section is northwest of Capitol Hill. This arrangement makes Capitol Hill the center of town, just as L'Enfant planned it some 200 years ago.

The four sections have separate personalities. They are not equal in size or in population. The Northwest section contains Washington's prime neighborhoods, including Georgetown and the Rock Creek Park vicinity. Northwest Washington embraces about half the city's land area and holds almost half its people. The White House, the Lincoln Memorial, and many of the Smithsonian museums stand in the Northwest section. The campuses of five universities are also in the Northwest. Elegant shops and the city's finest restaurants are located there, too.

Southwest Washington lies just south of Northwest quadrant. The two sections are separated by the National Mall. The Southwest is the smallest of the four sections, with only one-eighth of the city's land and about 4 percent of its people. Much of the Southwest was a poorer area in the 1930s and 1940s. Photographers often snapped pictures of its run-down shacks with the nearby Capitol dome in the background. In a massive urban renewal effort, Southwest Washington's dwellings were bulldozed and replaced by housing projects and attractive town houses.

Like much of Washington, the Southeast section is a neighborhood of contrasts. Near the Capitol are high-rise apartment buildings and restored older houses. The Capitol Hill region is one of the city's best. A highlight of the district is the Eastern Market, where farmers sell produce and flowers. However, the Southeast section is also the site of the Anacostia neighborhood, one

Anacostia is one of the city's poorest sections.

of the most impoverished in Washington. Anacostia suffered great damage during the 1968 riots, and the neighborhood is still struggling to restore itself.

Northeast Washington has both middle-class and low-income residents. The Northeast section has about one-fourth of the city's population and one-fourth of its land area. Howard University and the Catholic University of America are in the Northeast. Another highlight of the Northeast is the National Arboretum, which sprawls along the banks of the Anocostia River.

City streets are named in a definite pattern. Streets that run north and south are numbered—for example First and Second Street. Streets that go east and west are lettered—such as C Street and D Street. Many wide avenues are named for states: Pennsylvania Avenue, Rhode Island Avenue, and New York Avenue. The avenues intersect at celebrated crossings like Dupont Circle and Washington Circle. This pattern is broken in the Georgetown neighborhood, which predates Washington and retains some of its old street names.

Opposite: A residential area in Northwest Washington

CHAPTER SEVEN

The Government within a Government

The city of Washington was created to serve as the headquarters for the U.S. federal government. But does that mean the federal government has the right to decide what kind of trees should be planted along the boulevards? Should decisions regarding the city's internal affairs be made by local leaders or by representatives and senators from other states? This question has been argued in Washington for decades.

A view of Washington from Arlington

A City in Crisis

A 1996 report noted that only 30 percent of the murders committed in Washington are solved by the police department—less than half the national average. The police claim they lack the money to investigate crimes thoroughly. Some officers say they have to fill the gas tanks of their squad cars with their own money because the city so often runs out of funds.

Opposite: The Supreme Court building

In late 1997, hundreds of Washington's inner-city children found locked doors when they went to school. The children were turned away because the school buildings had leaky roofs and were said to be unsafe for classes. Several of the city's public schools date back to the 1880s and have gone without repair for years. Some schools fail fire inspections.

Local government officials say a shortage of money hampers their city. One-third of the city's funds come from the federal government. City politicians complain that federal authorities are willing to spend money on the Mall and in downtown where the tourists go, but they scrimp on funding projects in the inner city. Federal leaders counter by charging the city wastes money through its own inefficiency. One study pointed out that a large group of office workers employed by the municipal government did little more than collect the time cards of other city office workers.

Washington's local leaders have limited ability to tax residents and to spend money on projects they believe the city needs. The right of a city to run its own affairs is called home rule. Most other large cities in the nation enjoy home rule. In the capital, home rule has long been a subject of heated debate.

Home Rule—the Background

The Constitution says Congress shall have authority "to exercise exclusive Legislation in all Cases whatsoever" over the future "Seat of Government of the United States." Thus, from the beginning, Congress had the power to act as a sort of city council for the capital. As early as 1802, Congress allowed Washingtonians

Government Extravagance

Everyone complains about wasteful spending in Washington, but few leaders—either in the federal government or the municipal government—do anything to stop the practice. In 1998, the federal government completed a huge office building named for President Ronald Reagan. The building, 10 stories high and covering 10 acres (4 ha), is second in size only to the Pentagon. A handsome stone structure, it stands just two blocks from the White House in a complex called the Federal Triangle. But the problem is that this building cost the taxpayers almost $1 billion, about twice the estimated price when the project began. And the irony is that this enormous office complex is dedicated to Ronald Reagan, who, as president, promised to cut government spending. ■

to have a local government with a city council and a mayor. But city residents could not vote for members of Congress or for the president.

In 1874, Congress became furious when the city ran up huge debts on projects deemed to be wasteful—a complaint as modern as today. Congress stripped home-rule power from Washington residents and ordered that the city be run by a three-person commission. This made Washington the only city in the country whose citizens could not elect their own leaders. In 1964, a constitu-

Washington, D.C.'s Symbols

Washington, D.C., is not a state, even though many residents wish it would become one. Yet, like the states, the city values its very special symbols.

Bird: Wood thrush The wood thrush is a common North American bird noted for its pleasing, flutelike songs.

Tree: Scarlet oak A particularly handsome tree, the scarlet oak (left) grows throughout the eastern United States.

Flower: American beauty rose A favorite of Washington gardeners, the American beauty rose is given a prized place in many District gardens.

Washington, D.C.'s Mayors

Name	Party	Term
Walter Washington	Dem.	1975–1979
Marion Barry	Dem.	1979–1991
Sharon Pratt Dixon	Dem.	1991–1995
Marion Barry	Dem.	1995–1999
Anthony Williams	Dem.	1999–

District Flag and Seal

Adopted in 1938, the city's flag is based on George Washington's coat of arms; it has three red stars above two red stripes on a white field. Adopted in 1871, the official seal shows the figure of a woman representing Justice putting a wreath on George Washington's statue; in the background is the Potomac River. ■

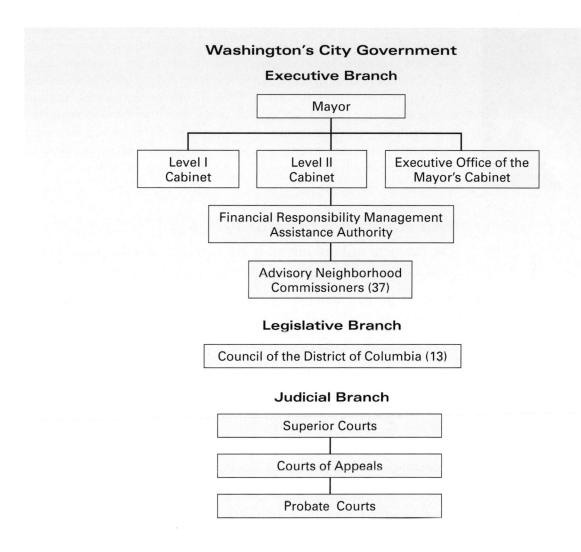

Washington's City Government

Executive Branch

Mayor

Level I Cabinet

Level II Cabinet

Executive Office of the Mayor's Cabinet

Financial Responsibility Management Assistance Authority

Advisory Neighborhood Commissioners (37)

Legislative Branch

Council of the District of Columbia (13)

Judicial Branch

Superior Courts

Courts of Appeals

Probate Courts

tional amendment gave city residents the right to vote in presidential elections. Then, in 1975, Congress allowed Washington to elect a mayor and a city council form of government. Twenty years later, Congress restricted home rule, and by the late 1990s the city was again run by a commission. Once more, Washingtonians had little say in their own government.

Marion Barry, Controversial Mayor

In 1978, Washingtonians elected Marion Barry as their mayor. A one-time civil rights worker, Barry appealed to African-Americans and to poor people. He was also a strong advocate of home rule, calling the city of Washington a "stepchild of government." In 1990, Barry was arrested for smoking crack cocaine in a Washington hotel room and was sentenced to six months in jail. Two years later, despite his drug conviction, he was elected to the city council, and two years after that he was reelected as mayor. Barry served as mayor for four terms before announcing his retirement in 1998. ■

The Capital's Economy

The business of Washington is government, and the federal government is by far its largest single employer. One in five workers in the metropolitan area has a government job. Washington has been called "the nation's biggest company town," and in this company town the federal government is the top boss.

However, thousands of Washingtonians work for private companies whose goal is to influence the course of government. These organizations include the Animal Welfare Institute, the American Association of Retired Persons, the National Wildlife Federation, and many others. Service institutions such as the Air Force Association and the Daughters of the American Revolution have headquarters in Washington. Educational and cultural groups including the American Association for the Advancement of Science, the National Academy of Sciences, the American Film Institute, and the American Theater Association are also located in the capital.

Washington has several other industries that employ many of its residents. Printing is the largest industry in the metropolitan area. The Government Printing Office runs several plants in the city.

The Bureau of Engraving and Printing

Every morning hundreds of tourists line up in front of Washington's Bureau of Engraving and Printing building to watch its most fabulous operation—the printing of cash. Presses in the building run nonstop, turning out $120 billion in greenbacks each year. Tour guides explain that the average dollar bill falls apart in just eighteen months, and the cash printed here replaces existing paper money.

As the wide-eyed visitors watch, giant sheets of thirty-two bills each roll off the presses in denominations of $1, $5, $10, $20, $50, and $100. All visitors observe this operation from behind thick glass panels, and no one is allowed to touch the merchandise. ■

Newsweek magazine and the *Washington Post* newspaper are also printed there. The *Washington Post* is considered one of the nation's best newspapers. Tourism is another important source of jobs. Each year, visitors spend about $2.4 billion in the city's hotels and restaurants, and some 60,000 Washingtonians work in tourist-related firms. Education is a large field, too, especially at the city's universities.

CHAPTER EIGHT

A Walk through the National Mall

Washington's historic neighborhoods are delightful places to walk through. Trees line the boulevards. Statues, fountains, and stately public buildings remind visitors that this is a city designed to inspire. The most popular walk of all is the 2-mile (3-km) trek down the National Mall, the heart of Washington, between the Capitol and the Lincoln Memorial.

The National Mall is the setting for celebrations and demonstrations.

The Capitol Hill Neighborhood

Begin a tour of Capitol Hill at Union Station, which is more like a palace than a train depot. The station's main hall has a 96-foot (29-m) arched ceiling bright with skylights. The statues that line its walls make the building look like it was designed for a Roman emperor—and indeed it was inspired by the Baths of Diocletian in ancient Rome. Completed in 1907, Union Station was revitalized by a $160 million restoration project in the 1980s. The station now has 100 restaurants and shops as well as a movie complex.

Next door to Union Station stands a building that served as the city's main post office until 1986. Today, it is the National Postal Museum and displays an intriguing collection of artifacts used over the ages by the U.S. Postal Service. From the ceiling hangs a flimsy-looking airplane flown decades ago by brave air-

Opposite:
Students in front
of the U.S. Capitol

Daniel Burnham, Architect of Grandeur

Union Station and the National Postal Museum were designed by Daniel Burnham, who once told a group of architectural students, "Make no small plans; they have no magic to stir men's souls." Born in 1846, Burnham was both an architect and a city planner. He served for a time on the city's Commission of Fine Arts. Washington's Union Station is one of his greatest creations. ■

mail pilots. Thousands of stamps are also on display. Another exhibit consists of a collection of unusual mailboxes, one of which was made out of a car muffler. Kids enjoy a video game that hearkens back to the 1850s and challenges players to get twenty bags of mail from Philadelphia to New Orleans via trains and stagecoaches.

In that 1939 movie *Mr. Smith Goes to Washington*, young Senator Smith says, "[There's] the Capitol dome—as big as life, sparkling away under that old sun out there." Over the years this great building has thrilled millions of visitors. The soaring dome, topped by the Statue of Freedom, rises 300 feet (91 m). One historian called the Capitol "the spirit of America in stone." Many of the building's 540 rooms are open to the public. The largest room is the Rotunda, a circular hall 95 feet (29 m) in diameter that lies directly under the dome. The Rotunda wall has eight enormous

The paintings along the Rotunda wall depict American history.

paintings depicting events in U.S. history, such as the reading of the Declaration of Independence. Statuary Hall inside the Capitol honors American heroes such as Daniel Webster and Henry Clay.

The Capitol is the majestic place where the Senate and the House of Representatives meet. The laws made at the meetings make the Capitol perhaps the most important building in the nation. A few steps east of the Capitol is the Supreme Court building, where laws are reviewed by nine black-robed justices. If the justices decide a law violates the U.S. Constitution, they have the power to reject that law. The Supreme Court hears an average of 500 cases a year. Visitors are allowed to watch the court at work. The opening ceremony begins when a marshall cries out, "Oyez, oyez, oyez," which means, "hear ye, hear ye" in French, and announces that the U.S. Supreme Court is in session. The Supreme Court building resembles a Greek temple. It was built in 1935 of glistening white marble, and its front entrance is lined with a double

Terror in the Capitol

July 24, 1998, seemed a typical day at the Capitol. Visiting Boy Scout troops posed for pictures and lines of tourists wound up the steps. Suddenly, a man dressed in khakis tried to run around the metal detectors. When Capitol police officer Jacob Chestnut attempted to stop him, the man fired a pistol at Chestnut. Another officer, John Gibson, returned fire. Tourists screamed, and parents fell down over their children to protect them from bullets. When the attacker was finally subdued, the two police officers lay dying and one tourist was severely wounded. The gunman, also wounded, was an Illinois resident with a history of mental problems. The two officers—Gibson and Chestnut—were buried with honors befitting U.S. heroes. ■

row of graceful columns. Inscribed above the columns are the words "Equal Justice under Law."

Also on Capitol Hill is the Library of Congress, the world's largest library. The Library of Congress holds more than 100 million items, including 26 million books. An up-to-date accounting of its holdings is difficult to take since the library acquires 400 new items every hour. One of its earliest acquisitions was the personal library of Thomas Jefferson consisting of 6,500 books. The library building opened in 1897, and many architectural experts say it is the most beautiful structure in the city.

On the southwest side of Capitol Hill is the United States Botanic Garden. Plants found in this delightful little park range from desert cacti to sweet-smelling orchids. A bubbling cast-iron fountain in the park was created by Frédéric Auguste Bartholdi, the

Capitol Hill is home to the United States Botanic Garden.

designer of New York's Statue of Liberty. The nearby Folger Shakespeare Library holds the world's largest collection of Shakesparean works, including 250,000 books, 100,000 of which are classified as rare. The public may view displays of the rare books, but only scholars and experts on the writings of William Shakespeare may use the library.

Museum Row

Walk down Capitol Hill and cross Third Street. Follow the National Mall and you will be flanked by museum buildings on your left and right, an expanse often called Museum Row. Nine of those buildings belong to the Smithsonian Institution and house more than 130 million articles. No city on Earth has a muscum complex that can match the National Mall.

Andrew Mellon, a wealthy patron of the arts

On your right are the two buildings that make up the National Gallery of Art. They offer a marvelous display of paintings by European masters such as Leonardo da Vinci, Raphael, Titian, El Greco, Claude Monet, and Vincent Van Gogh. Many of these masterpieces were acquired early in the twentieth century by Andrew Mellon, a member of a wealthy Pittsburgh banking and steel-producing family. Mellon served as secretary of the treasury in the 1920s. In 1937, he donated his substantial art collection, along with millions of dollars, to establish the now renowned National Gallery of Art.

On your left is the National Air and Space Museum, a celebration of the progress of flight. At the building's massive front door, the Wright brothers' first aircraft hangs above the *Apollo 11* space capsule. Only sixty-six years separated the first manned flight, which covered 120 feet (36 m), from the spectacular journey to the moon. Other milestone aircraft in the museum are the *Spirit of St. Louis*, which took Charles Lindbergh on the first solo flight across the Atlantic Ocean in 1927, and the space capsule *Friendship 7* in which John Glenn became the first American to orbit Earth in 1962. Each year this building receives more visitors than any other museum in the city. Expect to hear a lot of "ohhhhs" and "ahhhhs" as excited guests dash from exhibit to exhibit.

The National Air and Space Museum houses historic aircraft.

Senate Bean Soup

This soup is served in the Senate dining room and has become a Washington tradition.

Ingredients:

- 1 pound dried navy beans
- 1 ham hock
- 12 cups water
- 3 onions, chopped
- 3 celery stalks, chopped
- 2 cloves garlic, minced
- 1 teaspoon chopped parsley
- 1/2 pound potatoes, mashed
- salt and pepper to taste
- 1 teaspoon chopped green onions

Directions:

Wash the beans and place in a large bowl. Fill the bowl with enough water to cover the beans by 3 or 4 inches (8 or 10 cm). Remove any beans that float in the water. Soak the beans overnight and then drain.

Place 12 cups of water in a large pot. Add the beans and the ham hock and bring the water to a boil. Lower the heat and simmer, partially covered, for 2 hours. Skim off any foam that rises to the surface.

Add the onions, celery, garlic, parsley, and mashed potatoes to the pot and stir well. Simmer for another hour, or until the beans are tender.

Add the salt and pepper. Take the ham hock out of the soup and scrape off any meat. Put the meat back in the soup, and discard the bone.

Serve the soup with the chopped green onions as a garnish.

Serves 6.

A few steps away, the Hirshhorn Museum and Sculpture Garden houses one of the world's finest collections of modern art and sculpture. The drum-shaped building stands on thick posts and looks down on a delightful sculpture garden. This museum is the gift of Joseph H. Hirshhorn, a European immigrant who became a millionaire and donated 4,000 paintings and more than 2,000 sculptures to the Smithsonian. Next door is the Arts and Industries Museum, a 100th-birthday gift from the United States to itself. Opened in 1881—five years after the actual birthday—it displays state-of-the-art machinery and railroad equipment from that time. Today, the Arts and Industries Museum also features changing exhibits from the Anacostia Museum and the Center for African American History and Culture.

The very first Smithsonian museum building was completed on the Mall in 1855. It contained laboratories, a lecture hall, an art gallery, and a science museum. Now, it is home to the Smithsonian's administration offices and to a visitors center. Its official name is the Smithsonian Building, but it is commonly called the Castle, simply because it looks like one.

A lively world of art surrounds the historic Castle building. The National Museum of African Art is the country's greatest collection of artwork from sub-Saharan Africa. More than 7,000 African artifacts are displayed. The objects range from everyday bowls and baskets to intricately carved statues. The Arthur M. Sackler Gallery is dedicated to Asian art. Guests see Chinese jade figures made in 3000 B.C., and Near Eastern works in silver, gold, and bronze. The Freer Gallery of Art displays important paintings by the American artist James McNeill Whistler.

The U.S. Holocaust Memorial Museum

Slightly off the Mall stands a powerful reminder of Europe's World War II Holocaust. Enter the building and an attendant will give you the identity card of an actual Holocaust victim. By war's end there were more than 6 million such victims—Jews, Gypsies, the disabled, and anyone else the Nazi regime deemed unfit to live. See the haunting Tower of Faces (above), 1,500 family photos of people who suffered and died in the death camps. Follow Daniel's Story, the account of a German Jewish boy in the 1940s who went from a middle-class home to the horrors of the death camps. The Holocaust Memorial tells a sad story, but it also records the ultimate triumph of the human spirit. The museum's message is inscribed on its outside walls: "never again will the world stand silent, never again will the world . . . fail to act in time to prevent the terrible crime of genocide." ■

The National Archives

Set back from the Mall is the National Archives building, which holds important papers dating back to the 1700s. The Constitution, the Declaration of Independence, and the Bill of Rights are on display behind bulletproof glass. Sometimes called the "nation's memory," the National Archives also holds pleasant tidings of the country's past, such as old musical recordings and photos. In addition, the building contains reminders of grim periods in U.S. history by preserving the cargo manifestos of slave ships. ■

A stuffed African elephant, one of the largest ever found in modern times, greets visitors at the National Museum of Natural History. Watch out! The elephant looks like he is charging right at the museum's entrance. Giant skeletons dominate Dinosaur Hall,

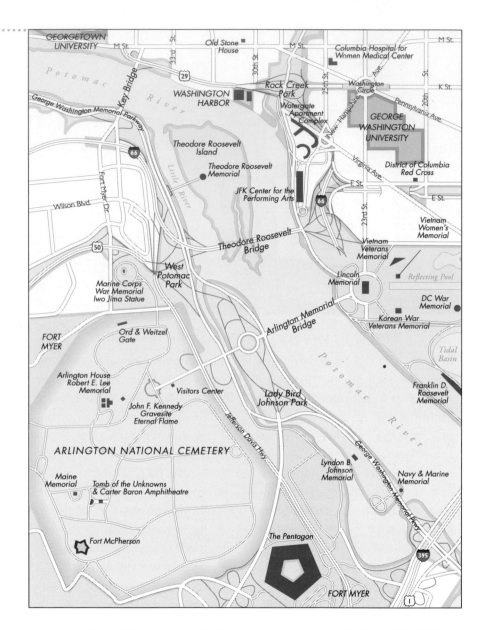

West of the National Mall

where a 70-million-year-old dinosaur egg is on display. The Life in the Ancient Seas exhibit features a 92-foot (28-m) model of a blue whale hanging from the ceiling. In 1996, a 4.5-billion-year-old rock from the planet Mars went on permanent display. The Mars rock came to Earth thousands of years ago as part of a meteor, and sci-

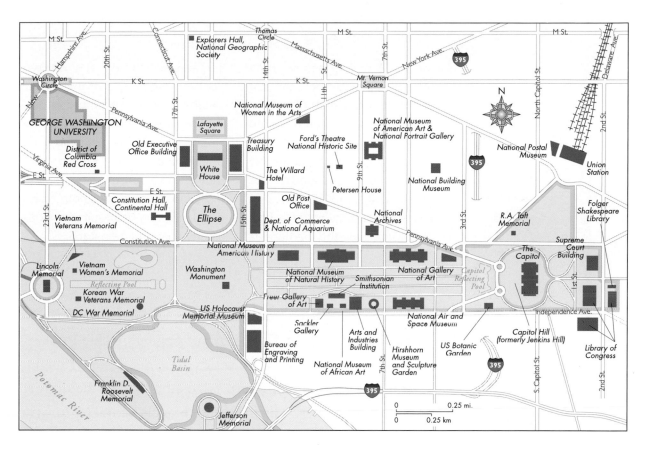

The National Mall

entists believe it contains evidence that life once existed on our neighboring planet. In all, some 120 million objects—from meteor fragments to moon rocks—are on exhibit in this wonderful museum.

The Smithsonian Institution's National Museum of American History is sometimes called the National Attic because so many household objects, old but still cherished, are stored there. The museum's stated purpose is to celebrate "everyday life in the American past." Guests see a cast-iron toy train and an early television set with a screen about as large as the face of a flashlight.

The Hope Diamond

Every year, 6 million people come to see the Hope Diamond, the star of the National Museum of Natural History. The largest blue diamond on Earth, it was donated to the Smithsonian in 1958. In its display case, the priceless diamond rotates under special lights designed to make it sparkle, showing off its special fire. Some say the diamond is cursed because several of its owners have died tragic or mysterious deaths. Marie Antoinette, the French queen who once owned the Hope Diamond, lost her head to the guillotine during the French Revolution. However, the Smithsonian Institution has enjoyed nothing but good luck since it acquired the dazzlingly beautiful gemstone. ■

Odd objects include George Washington's wooden teeth, the ruby slippers Dorothy wore in *The Wizard of Oz*, and Archie Bunker's favorite chair from the 1970s TV series *All in the Family*. Hanging on a wall is one of the museum's prize attractions—the original "Star-Spangled Banner" which inspired Francis Scott Key to write the words to the national anthem in 1814.

Timeless Monuments

When you leave Museum Row and cross 14th Street, you see the Washington Monument rising ahead. This west end of the National Mall is devoted to monuments that represent the pride of the nation.

The Washington Monument is the tallest building in the city and the tallest masonry structure in the world. At night it is gently bathed in floodlights. Along with the White House and the Capitol it is one of the city's most famous landmarks. You may join the lines of tourists and take a seventy-second elevator ride to the observation platform. When the monument was dedicated in 1885, a noisy steam-powered elevator took twenty minutes to reach the top. Many people preferred to make a laborious walk up the 897 steps because they regarded the elevator as a dangerous contraption. Walking up the steps is not allowed today, but you can walk down and see the 193 carved stones sent by various states and nations as the monument was built.

One of the most pleasant Washington walks is along the 2,000-foot (609-m)-long Reflecting Pool. This 160-foot (48-m) wide

Other D.C. Museums

Dozens of museums operate in Washington, D.C. The Smithsonian Institution runs fourteen museum buildings, including nine on the Mall and the National Zoo. Other museums include:

Capital Children's Museum Hands-on displays teach children about life in other countries and other cultures.

Corcoran Gallery of Art The oldest and largest private gallery in the United States has an excellent collection of American paintings.

Decatur House A restored 1819 house designed by Benjamin H. Latrobe, an important architect in the capital.

Hillwood Museum A luxurious 25-acre (10-ha) estate that once was home to Marjorie Merriweather Post of the Post cereal family.

National Museum of American Art A wonderful collection of American art through the ages.

National Aquarium Sea turtles, sharks, eels, and hundreds of other examples of marine life entertain visitors at the nation's oldest aquarium (established in 1873).

National Building Museum An array of blueprints and models explain the complex problems of construction.

National Museum of Women in the Arts Shows more than 1,500 works by women painters and sculptors.

National Portrait Gallery Contains statues and portraits of men and women who made significant contributions to the United States.

Navy Museum Missiles, cannons, and submarines are prominent in this museum which covers 200 years of U.S. Navy history.

The Renwick Gallery Features American arts and crafts including fine jewelry and furniture. ■

pool mirrors the long and narrow image of the Washington Monument. Sidewalks along the Reflecting Pool are tree-shaded, and ducks swim in the waters.

The walk leads to the Vietnam Veterans Memorial. Active U.S. involvement in the Vietnam War began in 1964 and ended in 1973. In 1982, the Vietnam Veterans Memorial was dedicated. Designed by student Maya Lin, it consists of a black granite wall where the names of more than 58,000 U.S. citizens killed or missing in the war are inscribed. Often you will see men and women study this

The Vietnam Veterans Memorial was dedicated in 1982.

V-shaped wall to find the name of a loved one killed in Vietnam. The undeclared war in Vietnam divided the nation almost as badly as the Civil War. The wall was designed to soothe bitter memories. Some people call it "the wall of healing."

For many years, few Americans recalled that 13,000 U.S. women served in Vietnam, and that eight died during the war. To serve as a reminder of their role, the Vietnam Women's Memorial was erected near the wall in 1993 as part of the Veterans Memorial. Sculpted by Glenna Goodacre, the monument consists of four bronze figures. Three servicewomen tend to a badly wounded soldier. One figure looks up to the sky, perhaps hoping to see an evacuation helicopter or perhaps asking for the help of God.

Near the Vietnam Veterans Memorial wall is the Vietnam Women's Memorial statue.

The Korean War (1950–1953) is sometimes called the Forgotten War. The bloody conflict was largely ignored by the public while it was being fought, and it is now a footnote rather than a chapter in the history books. But 55,000 American men and women were killed in Korea— almost as many as were killed in Vietnam. The war is presently remembered in the Korean War Veterans Memorial, dedicated in 1995. The memorial shows nineteen life-sized soldiers, covered

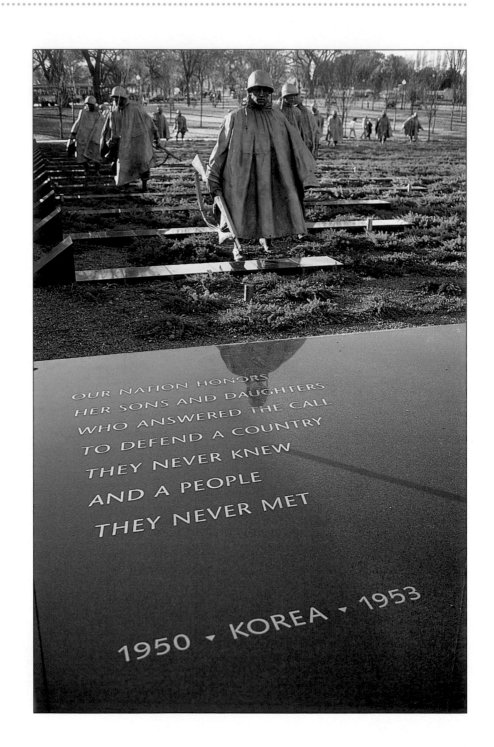

OUR NATION HONORS HER SONS AND DAUGHTERS WHO ANSWERED THE CALL TO DEFEND A COUNTRY THEY NEVER KNEW AND A PEOPLE THEY NEVER MET

1950 ▾ KOREA ▾ 1953

**The Korean War
Veterans Memorial**

by ponchos to fend off rain or sleet, walking cautiously toward an American flag. The figures are made of stainless steel. Their faces have a haunting look of both fear and determination. It is a fitting tribute—finally—to the veterans of the Forgotten War.

The National Mall is anchored by the beloved Lincoln Memorial. Here, the 19-foot (6-m) statue of Lincoln sits under a roof braced by thirty-six columns, which stand for the thirty-six states existing in 1865 when Lincoln was assassinated. Inscribed on the south wall is the Gettysburg Address, in which Lincoln asked his people to carry on the fighting in the Civil War. On the north wall are words from his second inaugural speech, when he appealed to the nation to bind the wounds of war and act, "With malice toward none, with charity for all." The Lincoln Memorial is the most emotional of all of Washington's commemorative statues. Some look at it and say Lincoln's face has a slight smile because he is happy that the great war is finally over. Others say he is brooding, terribly saddened by the war's bloodshed.

Monuments to Be

In the late 1990s, authorities in Washington announced plans for two future memorials. One memorial will honor the veterans of World War II and will stand near the Lincoln Memorial. The other will celebrate the life of Martin Luther King Jr. and will be constructed along the Mall between the Washington Monument and the Capitol. Supporters of Martin Luther King were pleased by the project, but many felt it should be closer to the Lincoln Memorial, the site of King's history-making "I have a dream" speech. ■

CHAPTER NINE

Other Attractions Near and Far

How many days, weeks, or even months does it take to see all the noteworthy sites in the Washington area? In truth it might take years because greater Washington offers so many exciting places to visit. During a brief stay it is a good idea to make a list of those must-see spots you surely don't want to miss. Here are some ideas for that list.

The White House

No trip to Washington is complete without at least an outside look at the president's house. It is probably the most frequently photographed residence in the world. TV news reporters are filmed with the White House in the background. Family groups are certain to pose for a picture in front of its gates. Its address—1600 Pennsylvania Avenue NW—is known to people living in the most remote corners of the earth. Over the years, the White House's outside appearance has been changed by various presidents and their wives. The south lawn today is shaded by majestic magnolia trees planted by President Andrew Jackson in the 1830s. First Lady Ellen Wilson started the famous Rose Garden in 1913. President Harry Truman added a balcony in 1948.

Long lines discourage many tourists from seeing the inside of

The State Dining Room is one of the White House rooms open to the public.

**Opposite:
Dumbarton Oaks**

What You Won't See in a White House Tour

Your chances of bumping into the president in the hallway while touring the White House are slim. The president's family lives in private quarters on the second floor where guests are not allowed.

Other White House sights you will not see include the indoor swimming pool built for Franklin Roosevelt, the basement air-raid shelter built during World War II, the bowling alley installed by Richard Nixon, and the jogging track put up by Bill Clinton. ■

the White House, but every year more than 1 million people brave the lines and take the one-hour tour. Only five rooms on the state floor, where official occasions are held, are open to the public—the State Dining Room, the Red Room, the Blue Room, the Green Room, and the East Room. On the ground floor, two rooms—the Vermeil Room and the Library—are open to the public. The State Dining Room is a spectacular setting that can accommodate up to 140 guests for dinner. Ever since the Jefferson Administration (1801–1809), presidents and their wives have used the Blue Room to receive guests. The delicate furniture displayed in the Blue Room was acquired by President James Monroe between 1817 and 1825. The Green Room is named for its light-green silk wall coverings. A unique feature of the Green Room is a revolving door dinner tray, sort of an eighteenth-century "lazy Susan," designed by Thomas Jefferson. The East Room is the biggest room in the White House. The prize of the East Room is the famous Gilbert Stuart portrait of George Washington rescued by Dolley Madison from torch-bearing soldiers during the War of 1812.

The Franklin D. Roosevelt and Thomas Jefferson Memorials

Franklin Roosevelt was the only president to be elected to four terms. He led the United States through the darkest days of the Great Depression in the 1930s and through most of World War II. He is honored in a lovely 7.5-acre (3-ha) site on the banks of the Potomac River. The memorial consists of four outdoor rooms that recall his four terms in office. The last term was shortened by his death in 1945. Sculptures include Roosevelt's wife, Eleanor, who was a crusader for the rights of African-Americans, women, and poor people. Also shown, to the delight of children, is a bronze statue of Roosevelt's dog, Fala, the president's constant companion in the White House.

A pleasant walk under the shade of cherry trees takes you from the Franklin Roosevelt Memorial to the Thomas Jefferson Memorial. The third president is known for many accomplishments, including writing the Declaration of Independence. Sculptures above the entrance show Jefferson working on the declaration along with Benjamin Franklin, John Adams, and others. The Jefferson Memorial was completed in 1943 when World War

The Franklin D. Roosevelt Memorial

Missing Wheelchair

Franklin Roosevelt contracted polio in 1921 when he was not quite forty years old. The disease left him without the use of his legs, dependent on a wheelchair. In Roosevelt's time, many people felt that a person who used a wheelchair was somehow not "manly" enough to be a political leader. Roosevelt almost never allowed himself to be photo-graphed in a wheelchair, even though it was well known he used one.

When the Roosevelt Memorial opened in 1997, no statue showed him in a wheelchair. This absence angered disability-rights groups. In 1998, the National Park Service announced it will add a wheelchair at the entrance of the memorial. ■

Defying the President's Wishes

About four years before he died, Franklin Roosevelt told Supreme Court Justice Felix Frankfurter that if a memorial to his presidency were built, it should be no larger than his desk. Today, the Roosevelt Memorial stretches the length of four football fields. ■

Take the Metro

Driving from place to place can be a nasty ordeal in Washington. Traffic jams are frenzied, and drivers unfamiliar with the city's layout get lost on the diagonal streets. A 1998 study ranked Washington second only to Los Angeles, California, as having the worst traffic congestion of any U.S. city. A much better way to get around is on the subway system, called the Metro. By the late 1990s, the Metro (which was in the process of expanding) had seventy-four stations and its tracks ran 89 miles (143 km). Rubberized tires on trains give passengers a smooth and quiet ride. The state-of-the-art Metro whisks people around the city and the suburbs much more efficiently than any form of surface transportation. In addition, the Metro is an architecturally stunning facility, not at all like the drab older subways in New York and Chicago. Washington's Metro stations have vaulted ceilings and lights tucked into complex honeycomb designs. Even waiting for a subway train can be an inspirational experience in Washington. ■

II consumed Washington. Despite pressing wartime priorities, President Franklin Roosevelt insisted that this testimonial to Jefferson be completed. Today, the circular building with fifty-four graceful columns is one of the city's most popular attractions.

The Washington National Cathedral

Turn a corner in what appears to be an ordinary Northwest Washington neighborhood and the twin towers of the Washington National Cathedral jump out at you. This vast church, built in the shape of a cross, is the sixth-largest cathedral in the world. Its outer walls are graced with intricate carvings. The rose window over its front door is made up of 10,500 pieces of stained glass. Construction on this great cathedral began in 1907. The building process continued for eighty-three years until the final stone was laid in September 1990. However, the church was open for worship long before its official completion date.

The Washington National Cathedral is the sixth-largest cathedral in the world.

Because of long traditions separating church and government there is no "national church" in the United States, but the Washington National Cathedral has served as a common place of worship for generations. Services to celebrate the ends of World War I and World War II were held here. Funerals for Presidents Wilson and Eisenhower were also held in the church. Wilson and his wife are buried on the grounds. Officially the church is Episcopalian, but people of all religions come to worship here. Tourists take in the array of stained-glass windows and statuary inside and walk through its 57-acre (23-ha) landscaped grounds.

Dumbarton Oaks

About 200 years ago, a lavish red-brick mansion in Georgetown was built by a Scottish family whose members had made a fortune in the tobacco business. The family named it Dumbarton Oaks after the Rock of Dumbarton in Scotland. In 1944, diplomats from around the world met there for the now-famous Dumbarton Oaks Conference. That conference led to the formation of the United Nations and gave Dumbarton Oaks its place in history.

Today, the building is owned by Harvard University and is used as a research facility. The building is also a museum showing splendid examples of ancient American art and artworks from the Byzantine period in Europe. Particularly interesting are jade figures of snakes crafted by Mayan artists more than 1,000 years ago. Many tourists come to see Dumbarton Oaks's magnificent gardens. Spreading over 16 acres (65 ha), the lawns are modeled after European palace grounds. The intriguing Pebble Garden is a shallow pool made from thousands of multicolored pebbles.

Rows of heroes at Arlington National Cemetery

Arlington National Cemetery

The U.S. government maintains 114 national cemeteries where war veterans are buried. But in the hearts of citizens, Arlington National Cemetery is the true resting place of heroes.

A Cavalcade of Luminaries

Men and women who served honorably in the U.S. armed forces are allowed to be buried at Arlington. A short list of luminaries at Arlington includes:

Omar Bradley (1893– 1981) (top) Known as the "GI's General" in World War II, he eased the strain of war on ordinary soldiers by giving them prompt mail service and decent chow.

Abner Doubleday (1819– 1893) The commander of troops at Fort Sumter, his men fired the first shots by the North during the Civil War; for generations Doubleday was credited with inventing the game of baseball, but today historians believe he had little to do with the game's development.

Virgil Grissom (1926–1967) (center) The first U.S. astronaut to make more than one space flight, Grissom was killed along with two crewmates when fire broke out on their Apollo spacecraft; Roger Chaffee, also buried at Arlington, died in the same accident.

Marguerite Higgins (1920– 1966) (bottom) The only woman reporter at the fighting fronts in the early stages of the Korean War, she won a Pulitzer Prize for her courageous writing from the war zone.

Joe Louis (1914–1981) World War II veteran and heavyweight champion of the world from 1937 to 1949, Louis had a longer reign than any other champion in the history of boxing. Many experts hail him as the best boxer in history.

Audie Murphy (1924– 1971) The most decorated U.S. soldier of World War II, he received twenty-four medals including the nation's highest military award, the Medal of Honor. After the war, Murphy had a long, successful career in motion pictures.

Robert Peary (1856–1920) Peary was a U.S. Navy officer and explorer who led a 1909 expedition that was first to reach the North Pole.

Walter Reed (1851–1902) Reed was an Army doctor whose experiments led to the treatment of typhoid and yellow fevers. ■

More than 250,000 men and women—veterans of every war the nation has fought—lie at the 612-acre (248-ha) site. Resting at Arlington are two presidents—John F. Kennedy and William Howard Taft. Also there are scores of army generals and admirals, thousands of privates and ordinary seamen, and several former slaves. Most of the honored dead are marked by simple gravestones with curved tops. Lines of such stones lace the grassy fields looking like soldiers standing at attention.

Crowds of tourists gather at Arlington's Eternal Flame which marks the grave of President John F. Kennedy, who served in the U.S. Navy in World War II. To the rear is the gravesite of Robert Kennedy, the president's brother and U.S. attorney general, who was assassinated in 1968. John Kennedy was a hero in World War II. It is less well known that his younger brother Robert served as an ordinary seaman shortly after the war.

A guard at the Tomb of the Unknowns

One of the most moving shrines at Arlington is the Tomb of the Unknowns, where unknown dead of World War I, World War II, and Korea are buried. The violence of war produces many unknowns—men whose bodies are so torn from bullets and shells that they cannot be identified. An unknown, being no one, can be anyone. Families who have lost a relative listed as "missing in action" can believe they have discovered their loved one here. Soldiers from the Third Army Infantry, called the Old Guard, perform an impressive and solemn Changing of the

Guards ceremony at the tomb. Words inscribed on a huge white marble block tell visitors: HERE RESTS IN HONORED GLORY AN AMERICAN SOLDIER KNOWN BUT TO GOD.

The Pentagon and the Iwo Jima Statue

Across the Potomac River from the capital stands the Pentagon. The five-sided building's mammoth scale reflects the enormity of its mission. The Pentagon is headquarters for the U.S. armed forces, the largest and most costly organization in the world. How big is this headquarters building? Consider a few facts: it has 17.5 miles (29 km) of hallways, enough telephone wire behind its walls to wrap around the earth two and a half times, and 283 rest

The size of the Pentagon is overwhelming.

This memorial depicts the raising of the U.S. flag at Iwo Jima.

rooms. The Pentagon is open to the public for guided tours, but children are reminded to stay close to their parents. One joke says that a little boy once got lost in the tangle of hallways and emerged twenty-five years later as an army general.

Iwo Jima is a tiny rock of an island that lies a few hundred miles off the coast of Japan. In 1945, it was the scene of a terrible World War II battle, as its Japanese defenders fought U.S. Marines for every inch of ground. After four days of bloody combat, a group of marines struggled to the peak of Mount Suribachi, the island's highest point. There they raised an U.S. flag while a photographer snapped a picture. The picture appeared on front pages in newspapers at home and inspired a war-weary public. Today, the flag-raising scene is immortalized in the dramatic bronze statue officially called the U.S. Marine Corps Memorial. Words on the base of the

Future Monuments, Eternal Controversy

In 1997, the Air Force Memorial Foundation announced plans to build a statue commemorating the air force. The problem? The new memorial was to be erected about 500 feet (152 m) downhill from the Iwo Jima statue. Marine veterans were enraged. They claimed the Air Force should build at another location so as not to distract from the Marine Corps site. Argument over monuments has a long history in the capital.

In the 1930s, a grove of cherry trees had to be cut down to build the Jefferson Memorial. Several Washington society ladies chained themselves to the trees in an attempt to save them from the ax. Even George Washington objected to a testimonial to himself. The first president thought that using taxpayer money to build the proposed Washington Monument was a terrible waste of public funds. ■

statue tell visitors that for the Marines on Iwo Jima: UNCOMMON VALOR WAS A COMMON VIRTUE.

Mount Vernon

About 16 miles (26 km) south of the capital spreads Mount Vernon, the estate of George Washington. The first president lived on these grounds for forty years. In the eight years when he was away fighting the Revolutionary War, Washington sent back detailed letters as to what repairs should be made on the house and what crops should be planted. In Washington's time, Mount Vernon was a vast plantation that spread over 8,000 acres (3,237 ha) and was tended by some 200 slaves. Today, the Washington estate is composed of about 500 acres (202 ha) spread on a bluff overlooking the Potomac River. Many guests visit there on special river-cruise boats.

Arlington House

On a commanding hill at Arlington National Cemetery stands the handsome Arlington House. From 1831 until 1861 it was the home of Robert E. Lee, his wife Mary Anna, and their children. When the Civil War began, Lee took charge of the Southern forces and never again returned to the home and farm he loved. Arlington House has been restored to look as it did when Lee and his family lived there. The front portico with its six thick columns is an outstanding feature of the house. Its hillside location gives visitors a sweeping view of Washington, D.C. ■

Visitors to Mount Vernon today walk through a recreation of the slave quarters as well as the restored Washington residence. Rooms inside the manor house are decorated and furnished as they were in the 1790s. Guides point out some of Washington's prized personal possessions, such as a globe he ordered from a London shop. The wretched conditions of slave life are not sugarcoated, but people are told that George Washington was considered an especially kind master. He did not sell children away from their families, and he taught slaves useful skills such as carpentry and masonry. To the rear of the house are the gravesites of George and Martha Washington as well as the slave burial grounds.

Opposite: George Washington lived at Mount Vernon for forty years.

CHAPTER TEN

Celebrating Life in the Capital

During times of war or international crises, Washingtonians live in the center of the storm. In emergencies the eyes of all the world focus on the capital city. Tension is an unpleasant part of life in Washington when there is strife in the world. It is no wonder that Washington residents have learned to relax with festivals, sports, and the arts. The capital is an exciting city. Day after day, some entertaining event brings people together to celebrate life in the headquarters of the nation.

The annual Easter egg roll on the White House lawn

The Capital's Festive Calendar

Celebrations turn with the seasons in Washington. As certain as summer follows spring, the capital will rock with parades and parties that are enjoyed by everyone in the city.

A popular springtime event is the White House Easter Egg Roll. On the big day, young children, toddlers, and their parents gather on the White House South Lawn to hunt for Easter eggs. The guests also participate in races that consist of rolling the eggs on the grass. Often the president and the first lady attend the Easter egg party. In late March, the Smithsonian Institution sponsors kite-flying contests at the foot of the Washington Monument. The National Cherry Blossom Festival, usually held in April, features

Opposite: July 4th fireworks over the Washington Memorial

Inauguration Day

Washington is the most political town in the nation. Therefore the beginning of a president's new term is a cause for celebration, at least for the winning political party. A presidential inauguration takes place in late January once every four years. The series of gala events begin with the inaugural parade on Pennsylvania Avenue. As millions watch on television, the president stands on the Capitol steps to take the oath of office. Next, the president makes an inaugural speech, which may set the tone for the coming administration. Finally, the president and his wife attend several gala inaugural balls where they dance the night away. The National Museum of American History displays a stunning collection of gowns worn by first ladies at these inaugural balls. ■

The yearly Frisbee contest attracts all kinds of participants.

a parade down Constitution Avenue. The Cherry Blossom Festival also includes the lighting of an 8-foot (2.5 m) Japanese lantern that stands near the Tidal Basin.

The Festival of American Folklife, held in June and early July, kicks off the summer season. Sponsored by the Smithsonian, the folklife fair presents activities ranging from Native American dancing to lively fiddlers from Appalachia. In August, the U.S. Army Band assembles at the base of the Washington Monument and gives a rousing performance of Tchaikovsky's *1812 Overture*. The firing of cannons climaxes this stirring work, and the cannons are set off courtesy of the U.S. Army Artillery. A Frisbee contest is hosted in

A Glorious Fourth

The Independence Day bash is the highlight of the year for Washingtonians. The citywide party begins as the National Independence Day Parade booms down Constitution Avenue. The parade features floats, a beautiful queen, and high school marching bands from around the nation. Volunteers in period uniforms set up a Revolutionary War campsite near the steps of the National Archives building. Men and women read the Declaration of Independence to the crowds. The evening ends with an outdoor concert and a spectacular fireworks display. ■

September by, appropriately enough, the National Air and Space Museum.

October and the fall season are launched with the Taste of D.C. During this affair, scores of the city's restaurants set up stands along Pennsylvania Avenue and in other neighborhoods, inviting people to fatten up. The White House Fall Garden Tour is a two-day event that allows people to tour the famous Rose Garden. Halloween is celebrated locally as neighborhood groups set up "fright nights" and costumed block parties. Veterans Day, November 11, is a solemn tribute to the nation's war dead. The major event of Veterans Day occurs when the president or a high government official goes to Arlington National Cemetery to lay a wreath on the Tomb of the Unknowns.

Merry Christmas to All

On an evening in December, the president walks out to the Ellipse, an oval-shaped park next door to the White House. There, to the accompaniment of an orchestra and several choirs, he lights the National Christmas Tree. The tree-lighting signals the beginning of a two-week celebration called the Pageant of Peace. Night after night, carolers or a band bring holiday joy to the Ellipse as they wish a Merry Christmas to all. ■

National Park Service rangers paying tribute on Martin Luther King Jr.'s birthday in 1999

Winter in Washington is heralded by a special Christmas open house party at the Washington National Cathedral. Families come to the cathedral and enjoy an evening of caroling, bell-ringing, and a visit from St. Nick. In January, Martin Luther King Jr. birthday celebrations include speeches by civil rights leaders and a wreath-laying at the Lincoln Memorial. Black History Month in February reminds the country of African-American contributions to national culture. George Washington's birthday on February 22 brings celebrations at the Washington Monument and Mount Vernon.

The Sports Scene

Washingtonians love playing sports and watching sports contests. Amateur athletes as well as weekend spectators contribute to a spirited sports scene in the capital.

There are 45 public swimming pools in the District and 144 outdoor tennis courts. Inner-city basketball courts are always full of kids. Forty varieties of fish in the Potomac River lure fishing enthusiasts. Rock Creek Park offers horseback riding, calisthenics, and jogging, as well as an eighteen-hole golf course. Ice skating is fun on the Reflecting Pool, especially at night when the pool is illuminated.

It is impossible to determine how many bicycles are in use in the D.C. area, but you see them everywhere. Tourists unfamiliar with the city should beware of cycling on the traffic-clogged streets.

What's in a Team Name? Hoyas? Wizards?

"What's a Hoya?" is one of the most frequently asked questions by those unfamiliar with Georgetown University. Years ago, the school's sports teams were called the Stonewalls. But when students began a chant in Latin— *Hoya Saxa!* —the nickname Hoyas was born. Washington's pro basketball team used to be called the Bullets. In 1996, the name was changed to the Wizards because many people believed "Bullets" contributed to the capital's negative image as a crime-plagued city. ■

Washington residents, on the other hand, know the bike paths and use bicycles to beat the traffic. It is even permissible to take a bike on the city subway—the Metro.

The capital's most successful sports franchise—and its most passionately followed—is the Washington Redskins of the National Football League (NFL). The Redskins have won three Super Bowls—in 1983, 1988, and 1992. Fans will always remember the dramatic 1988 Super Bowl, in which Washington quarterback Doug Williams became the first African-American quarterback to lead his team to an NFL championship. In this very political city, however, the concept of political correctness is always near the surface. Many people around the country object to the name "Redskins" because they believe it belittles Native Americans.

While Washington is a football town, basketball runs a close

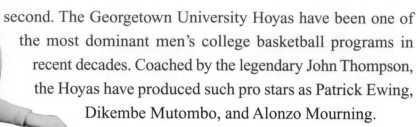

Pitcher Walter "Big Train" Johnson of the Washington Senators

second. The Georgetown University Hoyas have been one of the most dominant men's college basketball programs in recent decades. Coached by the legendary John Thompson, the Hoyas have produced such pro stars as Patrick Ewing, Dikembe Mutombo, and Alonzo Mourning.

On the pro side, the Washington Wizards are the capital's representatives in the National Basketball Association (NBA). City dwellers still talk about the franchise's one NBA championship, in 1978, when the team was led by the undersized but tough center Wes Unseld (now a member of the Basketball Hall of Fame). The Wizards share their home, the MCI Center sports arena, with the Washington Capitals of the National Hockey League (NHL). An NHL mainstay since their formation in 1974, the Caps had their best season ever in 1997–1998, when they won the Eastern Conference before losing the Stanley Cup Finals in Detroit.

Ask most young baseball fans today about Washington's baseball team and they'll give you a blank stare. But for most of a century, major-league baseball had a home in the capital. From 1901 to 1960, the Senators (also called the Nationals) were Washington's American League team before they moved to Minnesota to become the Twins. A new franchise called the Senators was quickly established, but the capital's heart was broken again when *that* team became the Texas Rangers after thc 1971 season. Now most of the city's fans follow the Baltimore Orioles. The city's professional soccer team, D.C. United, won championships in the late 1990s. Citizens of European and Latino heritage love soccer and fill the stands for every one of D.C. United's games.

The Lively Arts

Among the most entertaining free music shows in Washington are the Friday night performances of the Marine Band put on at the Marine Barracks at Eighth and Eye Streets, SE. The band is the pride of the corps, but its members are not marines. Instead, its 148 players are professional musicians chosen for their skill at their

The John F. Kennedy Center for the Performing Arts

Music and theater come magically together at the Kennedy Center, which opened in 1971. The theater and concert hall complex serves as the nation's cultural hub where the finest symphonies and dramas are presented. Its opera house seats 2,300 people for opera, ballet, or musical comedy. The National Symphony Orchestra performs at the center's concert hall. Pianists, chamber orchestras, and jazz groups entertain audiences at the Kennedy Center's Terrace Theater. Plays are put on at the Eisenhower Theater within the complex. A very popular children's theater also operates at the Kennedy Center. ■

Duke Ellington

Jazz is the United States's great contribution to the world of music. Over the years, African-American musicians have been leaders of the jazz movement. Probably the greatest of these was Duke Ellington (1899–1974). Born in Washington, Ellington wrote jazz classics such as "Creole Rhapsody" and "Reminiscing in Tempo" as well as such popular songs as "Mood Indigo" and "Solitude." Ellington was an outstanding ambassador of jazz, constantly traveling around the world and giving concerts to wildly enthusiastic audiences. ■

instruments and their talents in precision marching. For 200 years, the Marine Band has been a Washington tradition, performing at every presidential inaugural since that of Thomas Jefferson. From 1880 to 1892, the Marine Band was led by Washington-born John Philip Sousa. Known as the March King, Sousa wrote many stirring march pieces including "The Stars and Stripes Forever."

Music charms the capital year-round. During the summer months, the army, the air force, and the navy bands give free concerts. The city's Carter Baron Amphitheater hosts jazz and popular music concerts. In wintertime the National Symphony Orchestra performs at the Kennedy Center. The National Gallery of Art and the Library of Congress put on smaller-scale concerts.

Lovers of live theater consider Washington second only to New York in the number and quality of its theatrical productions. The National Theater has been staging plays since 1835, making it the third-oldest continuously operating theater in the country. Ford's Theatre was closed as a theater for more than a century after Lincoln's assassination there. Then, in 1968, Ford's reopened as both a working theater and as a museum commemorating the shocking murder. The Source Theater Company puts on Washington's newest plays. The Shakespeare Theater offers works by Shakespeare as well as many other beloved classics.

Visitors find drama in Washington simply by strolling the Mall and the many streets where a sense of history is everywhere. All they need to do is recall past events and think of the city as a theater that, through the years, has staged some of the most exciting events ever to take place in the United States.

The Lincoln Memorial is perhaps the capital's most passionate historical site. It was here that Marian Anderson broke the nation's hardest hearts with her singing, and it was here that Martin Luther King Jr. challenged the country to share his dream. Walk up the steps to the seated statue of Lincoln. Jefferson Smith took such a walk in that long-ago movie and said, "Mr. Lincoln, there he is, just looking right straight at you as you come up those steps." At the top, visitors stand with their backs toward Lincoln and gaze out at the Reflecting Pool, the Washington Monument, and the Capitol dome, feeling the spirit of Washington, the nation's capital.

Timeline

United States History

The first permanent English settlement is established in North America at Jamestown. **1607**

Pilgrims found Plymouth Colony, the second permanent English settlement. **1620**

America declares its independence from Britain. **1776**

The Treaty of Paris officially ends the Revolutionary War in America. **1783**

The U.S. Constitution is written. **1787**

The Louisiana Purchase almost doubles the size of the United States. **1803**

The United States and Britain **1812–15** fight the War of 1812.

Washington, D.C., History

1789 Congress decides that Federal City will be built on the border of Maryland and Virginia on the Potomac River.

1790 President George Washington appoints Pierre Charles L'Enfant to oversee plans for Federal City.

1792 Construction of President's House begins.

1793 The Capitol is completed.

1800 Federal City officially becomes the nation's capital.

1801 Federal City is renamed the City of Washington in honor of George Washington.

1814 British troops arrive in Benedict, Maryland, and begin marching toward Washington. Troops burn the President's House and the Capitol.

1817 The President's House is rebuilt and becomes known as the White House.

1829 James Smithson dies, donating his fortune to the city.

United States History

The North and South fight **1861–65** each other in the American Civil War.

The United States is **1917–18** involved in World War I.

The stock market crashes, **1929** plunging the United States into the Great Depression.

The United States **1941–45** fights in World War II.

The United States becomes a **1945** charter member of the U.N.

The United States **1951–53** fights in the Korean War.

The U.S. Congress enacts a series of **1964** groundbreaking civil rights laws.

The United States **1964–73** engages in the Vietnam War.

The United States and other **1991** nations fight the brief Persian Gulf War against Iraq.

Washington, D.C., History

1863 Slavery becomes officially illegal in Washington.

1865 President Abraham Lincoln is shot in Ford's Theatre on April 14.

1885 The Washington Monument is dedicated on February 21.

1897 The Library of Congress is completed.

1907 Union Station opens.

1922 The Lincoln Memorial is dedicated on May 30.

1932 World War I veteran "bonus marchers" arrive in Washington, demanding bonuses for their service during the war.

1939 African-American contralto Marian Anderson is not allowed to sing in Constitution Hall because she is black. She gives her concert at the Lincoln Memorial to an audience of 75,000.

1963 Martin Luther King Jr. delivers his "I have a dream" speech on August 28 at the National Mall.

1967 Antiwar protesters stage the March on the Pentagon.

Fast Facts

The Capitol

Founding date	Became the nation's capital in 1800
Origin of name	In honor of President George Washington
Nickname	The Nation's Capital, Capital City
Motto	*Justitia Omnibus* ("Justice for All")
Bird	Wood thrush
Flower	American beauty rose
State tree	Scarlet oak
Total area; rank	68 sq. mi. (177 sq km); 51st
Land; rank	61 sq. mi. (158 sq km); 51st
Water; rank	7 sq. mi. (18 sq km); 51st
Inland water; rank	7 sq. mi. (18 sq km); 51st
Geographic center	Near Fourth and L Streets, NW
Latitude and longitude	Washington, D.C., is located approximately between 38° 50′ and 39° 00′ N and 76° 50′ and 77° 10′ W

Scarlet oak

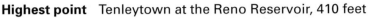

Under the Arlington Memorial Bridge

Highest point	Tenleytown at the Reno Reservoir, 410 feet (125 m) above sea level
Lowest point	Potomac River, 1 foot (.3 cm) above sea level
Population; rank	606,900 (1990 census); 49th
Population distribution	100% urban

Ethnic distribution (does not equal 100%)

African-American	66.0%
White	32.0%
Hispanic	6.0%
Asian and Pacific Islanders	3.0%
Native American	0.2%

Record high temperature	106° F (73°C) on July 20, 1930
Record low temperature	–15° F (–26 °C) on February 11, 1988
Average July temperature	78° F (26°C)
Average January temperature	37°F (3°C)
Average annual precipitation	50 inches (127 cm)

The White House

Natural Areas and Historic Sites

The White House, the most famous residence in the country, is maintained by the National Park Service and is open to visitors on most days.

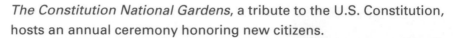

The Jefferson
Memorial

The Constitution National Gardens, a tribute to the U.S. Constitution, hosts an annual ceremony honoring new citizens.

Ford's Theatre, where Abraham Lincoln was assassinated, holds tours and is still a place where plays are performed.

The Frederick Douglass National Historic Site is the nineteenth-century home of the humanitarian and leader in the civil rights movement.

Pennsylvania Avenue National Historic Site is the part of the avenue between the Capitol and the White House, including Ford's Theatre.

National Parks

The Rock Creek Park, established in 1890, is one of the oldest wooded urban parks in the United States. Visitors can also see the Old Stone House, Washington's oldest house, located in Georgetown.

National Memorials

The Franklin Delano Roosevelt Memorial is dedicated to the country's thirty-second president and has four outdoor rooms, representing his four terms in office.

The Jefferson Memorial, like Monticello, his home in Virginia, resembles the Roman Pantheon. It stands next to the Tidal Basin, surrounded by Japanese flowering cherry trees.

The Lincoln Memorial honors the sixteenth president of the United States, and has the famous statue of a seated Lincoln looking down at visitors as they approach.

Lyndon Baines Johnson Memorial Grove on the Potomac has 500 white pine trees with inscriptions relating to the thirty-sixth president.

Theodore Roosevelt Island is a natural memorial to the country's twenty-sixth president.

The Vietnam Veterans Memorial includes the Vietnam Women's Memorial and honors the U.S. soldiers who died during the Vietnam War.

The Vietnam Veterans
Memorial

National Monument
The Washington Monument is one of the city's most recognized monuments. It is 555 feet (169 m) tall and has an observatory at the top.

National Historical Park
The Chesapeake and Ohio Canal—along the Potomac River, from Cumberland, Maryland, to Washington, D.C.,—is a memorial to the importance of transportation in the history of the United States.

National Scenic Trail
The Potomac River National Scenic Trail is a 704-mile (1,133-km) path joining parts of Pennsylvania to the tidewater area of the Potomac. It also includes the Mount Vernon Trail and the C&O Canal.

Sports Teams

NCAA Teams (Division 1)
American University Eagles

George Washington University Colonials

Georgetown University Hoyas

Howard University Bison

National Basketball Association
Washington Wizards

National Football League
Washington Redskins

National Hockey League
Washington Capitals

Major League Soccer
D.C. United

Women's National Basketball Association
Washington Mystics

The Washington Monument

At a Frisbee Contest

The U.S. Holocaust
Memorial Museum

Cultural Institutions

Libraries

The Library of Congress, founded by Thomas Jefferson in 1800, is the official library of the United States, serving the U.S. Congress, other parts of government, and the general public.

The Martin Luther King Memorial Library, the main building of the District of Columbia Public Library, has a large mural depicting the life of Dr. Martin Luther King Jr. and his influence on the African-American equal-rights movement.

The Folger Shakespeare Library contains the world's largest collection of information about William Shakespeare along with his works.

Museums

The Smithsonian Institution is a group of government museums and research centers that includes the Arthur M. Sackler Gallery, the Freer Gallery of Art, the Hirshhorn Museum and Sculpture Garden, the National Air and Space Museum, the National Museum of African Art, the National Museum of American Art, the National Museum of American History, the National Museum of the American Indian, the National Museum of Natural History, the National Portrait Gallery, the National Zoological Park, and the Renwick Gallery of the National Museum of American Art.

The U.S. Holocaust Memorial Museum is dedicated to providing information on the Holocaust and the millions of men, women, and children killed by the Nazis during World War II.

The National Museum of Women's History honors women throughout the history of the world.

Performing Arts

Washington, D.C., has two opera companies, two symphony orchestras, two dance companies, and two professional theater companies.

Howard University

Universities and Colleges
In the mid-1990s, the city had one public and seventeen private institutions of higher learning.

Annual Events

January–March
Three Kings Day Celebration (January 3)

Dr. Martin Luther King Jr.'s Birthday (January 15)

Chinese New Year Parade (January or February)

Abraham Lincoln's Birthday Celebration (February 12)

George Washington's Birthday Celebration (February)

Frederick Douglass Birthday Tribute (February)

Colonial Days at Mount Vernon (February–March)

D.C. Spring Antiques Fair (March)

Harambee Carnival (March)

Smithsonian Kite Festival (March)

St. Patrick's Day Parade (March 17)

April–June
Annual Montpelier Spring Festival (Spring)

Annual White House Easter Egg Roll (March or April)

National Cherry Blossom Festival in the Tidal Basin (April)

ZooFari (May)

Annual Capital Jazz Fest (June)

Annual National Capital Barbecue Battle (June)

Festival of American Folklife (June–July)

July–September
Hispanic Festival (summer)

July 4th celebration

The Easter egg roll

Fourth of July Fireworks Display

Annual Capital Soulfest (July)

Latin American Day Festival (July–August)

Annual Washington International Book Fair (September)

The Colonial Fair at Mount Vernon (September)

International Children's Festival (September)

A Taste of the Old Country in the Big City (September)

October–December

Taste of D.C. (October)

Fall Harvest Family Days (October)

Columbus Day Parade (October 12)

National Christmas Tree Lighting (December)

Washington Jewish Film Festival (December)

Famous People

Duke Ellington

Edward Albee (1928–)	Playwright
Bailey Kelly Ashford (1873–1934)	Soldier and surgeon
Clara Barton (1821–1912)	Civil War nurse, founder of American Red Cross
Alexander Graham Bell (1847–1922)	Inventor
David Brinkley (1920–)	Journalist and commentator
Art Buchwald (1925–)	Columnist
Frances Hodgson Burnett (1849–1924)	Novelist and playwright
Connie Chung (1946–)	Journalist
John Foster Dulles (1888–1959)	Statesman
Andrew Ellicott (1754–1820)	Surveyor
Duke Ellington (1899–1974)	Jazz composer and pianist
Edward Miner Gallaudet (1837–1917)	Educator

Henry Gannett (1846–1914)	Geographer and cartographer
Marvin Gaye (1939–1984)	Singer and songwriter
Leon Allen "Goose" Goslin (1900–1971)	Professional baseball player
Gilbert Hovey Grosvenor (1875–1966)	Geographer
Patricia Roberts Harris (1924–1985)	Lawyer and political official
Stanley Raymond "Bucky" Harris (1896–1977)	Professional baseball player and manager
Goldie Hawn (1945–)	Actor
J. Edgar Hoover (1895–1972)	FBI director
Jesse Jackson (1941–)	Clergyman and political activist
Pierre Charles L'Enfant (1754–1825)	French engineer and artist
George Preston Marshall (1896–1969)	Football executive
Mark Russell (1932–)	Humorist
Antonin Scalia (1936–)	Supreme Court justice
John Philip Sousa (1854–1932)	Composer and bandmaster
George Washington (1732–1799)	U.S. president and general
Woodrow Wilson (1856–1924)	U.S. president

George Washington

To Find Out More

History

- Davis, James E. *Washington, D.C.* World Cities series. Milwaukee: Raintree Press, 1990.

- Hilton, Suzanne. *A Capital City*. New York: Atheneum, 1992.

- Kent, Deborah. *The Lincoln Memorial*. Cornerstones of Freedom series. Danbury, Conn.: Children's Press, 1996.

- Kent, Deborah. *The Vietnam Women's Memorial*. Cornerstones of Freedom series. Danbury, Conn.: Childrens Press, 1995.

- Reef, Catherine. *Washington, D.C.* A Downtown America book. New York: Macmillan, 1990.

- St. George, Judith. *The White House: Cornerstone of a Nation*. New York: G. P. Putnam's Sons, 1990.

- Stein, R. Conrad. *The Arlington National Cemetery*. Cornerstones of Freedom series. Danbury, Conn.: Children's Press, 1995.

Biographies

- Ferris, Jeri. *What Are You Figuring Now? A Story about Benjamin Banneker*. Creative Minds series. Minneapolis: Carolrhoda Books, 1988.

Websites

■ **The Library of Congress**
http://www.loc.gov
To access information on
events at the library and
information on its many
holdings

■ **The Smithsonian
Institution**
http://www.si.edu
Links users to various divi-
sions of the museum

■ **U.S. House of
Representatives**
http://www.house.gov
For information on activities
in the House along with
information on your
representative

■ **U.S. Senate**
http://www.senate.gov
For information on activities
in the Senate along with
information on your senator

■ **Washington, D.C., Official
Tourism Website**
http://www.washington.org
Provides information on the
area's events and places to
visit

Addresses

■ **The U.S. Supreme Court**
1 First Street, NE
Washington, D.C. 20543
To contact the highest court
in the United States

■ **The White House**
1600 Pennsylvania Avenue,
NW
Washington, D.C. 20500
To send letters to the First
Family

Index

Page numbers in *italics* indicate illustrations.

Meet the Author

R. Conrad Stein was born and grew up in Chicago. As a teenager he served in the Marine Corps and then attended the University of Illinois, where he graduated with a degree in history. He is a full-time writer of material for young readers and has published more than 100 books. Stein lives in Chicago with his wife and their daughter, Janna.

The author first visited Washington, D.C., when he was a nineteen-year-old marine. Although he had little formal training in history at that point in his life, Stein was still inspired by the city's monuments and its ornate public buildings. Later Stein studied history. Knowledge of history made his return visits to Washington even more fascinating. Stein has toured Washington, D.C., at least a dozen times. At each visit he tries to see several new sights. Washington, D.C., is his favorite city to simply walk around in and feel the spirit of the nation.

In the summer of 1998, the Stein family made a special trip to the nation's capital. Mr. Stein was delighted to show his fifteen-year-old daughter Janna (left) and her friend, Bethany Suwinski (right), the highlights of Washington. Joining thousands of other tourists they visited the Smithsonian, the National Mall, the Jefferson and Roosevelt Memorials, and the Arlington National

Cemetery. At the Lincoln Memorial, Janna Stein took the top picture of the author with the Washington Monument in the background. Stein lives with his wife Deborah Kent (center) and daughter Janna in Chicago.

Photo Credits